REVIEWS OF "ABIDE IN ME"

As one of the first to read this book prior to its release, I would highly recommend it – whether you may be in a prison, hospital, care home, your workplace or your home, and whether you may be a practicing or non-practicing Christian, a non-believer, or even of another faith. God's message in the Holy Scriptures is meant for all, especially useful in surviving and enduring in what some ominously call the "post-Christian" era, in which the lasting, saving message of Jesus Christ becomes increasingly scorned, ignored, and challenged by the forces of the wicked. Reading these Scripture verses along with the reflections and prayers, are sure to inspire you to improve, and be truly worthy of God's creation.

Ralph Watzke, B.A., LL.B.,
Regina, Saskatchewan, Canada

Abide IN ME

366 Daily Devotional Readings

ELVIS A. IGINLA

ABIDE IN ME
366 DAILY DEVOTIONAL READINGS

iUniverse books may be ordered through booksellers or by contacting:

iUniverse
1663 Liberty Drive
Bloomington, IN 47403
www.iuniverse.com
1-800-Authors (1-800-288-4677)

ISBN: 978-1-4917-8215-6 (sc)
ISBN: 978-1-4917-8214-9 (hc)
ISBN: 978-1-4917-8213-2 (e)

Print information available on the last page.

iUniverse rev. date: 12/07/2015

DEDICATION

"There is no greater love than this: that a man lay his life down for his friends." At the prime of His life Jesus of Nazareth did exactly this and in so doing carved a path for me to know the true God and to become reconciled to God. The religion of Jesus teaches me how to love others and how to accept the grace and forgiveness of God. It is therefore to Jesus that I owe all that is good in me and it is to Jesus that I dedicate these readings.

ACKNOWLEDGMENTS

I thank my friend Ralph Watzke for reading through the book to identify typos and duplications of verses and I thank my dear wife Twyla, for reading through it several times, despite my protests.

January 1

*Like newborn infants, long for the pure, spiritual milk,
so that by it, you may grow into salvation.*

1 Peter 2:2

Reflection: The idea of a new birth for each of us is a theme that runs through the Bible. Christianity owes many of its practices to Judaism; after all, the early followers of Jesus, including eleven of His Apostles, had Jewish backgrounds. But Christian rebirth, signified by baptism, goes beyond the Jewish practice of washing or immersing in water before prayers. Christian baptism occurs once in a lifetime. A new birth occurs after we repent and accept the grace of God. This is spiritual rebirth. The verse above draws attention to the fact that our Christian journey can be compared to the birth of a new child. How a newborn turns out later in life depends partly on parenting and on the environment. The first few years of life teach a child about the consequences of behavior. Afterwards, the child becomes an adult and can then decide on which path to take. An adult who wishes to become a new creation, and to renounce the wickedness that became a part of her life as she grew older, is then baptized into the body of Christ (as practiced by those Protestant churches that teach adult baptism only). Infants that are baptized in the Catholic, Anglican, and a number of other Churches, are confirmed later on in life.

Prayer: Father God, feed me Your spiritual milk so that I may have Your attributes as I mature spiritually. May I always honor my baptism.

January 2

Therefore, I tell you, do not worry about your life, what you will eat or drink, or about your body, what you will wear.....

Matthew 6:25

Reflection: Jesus in this passage is not asking us to be lazy. On the contrary Jesus was a tireless worker and we are called to follow in His footsteps. While the Lord desires that we move from juvenile attitudes to a mature attitude, at each stage in life, we are never alone. If things are tight for us, or if we find ourselves barely getting by, there is a good reason for this. And so we need to double our efforts to understand what the Holy Spirit is trying to teach us. If we have questions about life or anything else, Jesus invites us to ask God. But when we bring questions to the Father we should be prepared to listen to His response. The only worry that we should have in life is about the choices we make.

Prayer: Spirit of God, help me always to understand what stands in the way of the things I desire and help me to use whatever gifts You give me with love and humility.

January 3

Nevertheless, I will bring health and healing to it; I will heal my people and will let them enjoy abundant peace and security.

Jeremiah 33:6

Reflection: This is the type of verse that brings tears to one's eyes. It highlights the depth of God's love for us. There are reasons why we fall ill. But whatever may be the source of our illness, our Father cares to discuss it with us. What type of prayer do we utter to the Lord when we are ill or in trouble? Is it God's anger that brought us illness? Is the illness a part of God's plan for us and for those around us? Is it something we ate? Are we deficient in vitamins and minerals? The first thing we should do in illness is pray and seek help from professional people. Prayer will help us understand whether there is a spiritual connection to our illness and even if this is not the case, we pray knowing that God is able to cure us or to direct us to those who could cure us. The same God that gave us His Spirit also made our body and as Jesus demonstrated several times, God can heal the physical body as well as the spirit.

Prayer: Father, please teach me about all the hidden things in my heart so that I will know myself and know the things which bring me pain. Help me to always understand any lessons that pain has to teach me about how I live my life and when I am ill, direct me to those who have the knowledge to help me.

January 4

---◦◦◦---

Blessed are the peacemakers for they will be called children of God.

Matthew 5:9

Reflection: Practical Christianity is about applying Christian principles in our daily lives. And God certainly wants us to live in peace. Some people broker peace while others take sides and fuel conflicts. Jesus does not call us to appease evil doers but He calls us to be honest brokers so that both sides in a dispute can feel the love of God and can then relent in their disagreement. History shows that in many cases, taking sides prolongs conflicts and increases casualties. Peacemakers who come as ambassadors for Christ are priceless. Jesus was a man of peace and He has called us to follow in His footsteps.

Prayer: Spirit of God, let me bring peace where there is discord, and may I not be partial in mediating other people's disputes.

January 3

Wickedness is folly and foolishness is madness.
Ecclesiastes 7:25

Reflection: Wickedness is being harsh with people and treating them with disrespect and less than how we would want to be treated. Wickedness creates enemies and takes away our peace of mind. No one likes a wicked inconsiderate person and people cheer whenever that person runs into difficulties. Wickedness attracts violence and so it is ultimately destructive. Wicked people never last, and wicked cultures never last. This is why it is foolish to persist in wickedness. Deep down, everyone wants to be liked and to be well thought of. Love warms people to us and so it is madness to persist in a behavior that we know brings us into disrepute. The Christianity that Jesus exemplifies is a respectful religion.

Prayer: Holy Spirit, teach me how to regain control of myself so that I will not be a foolish person and I will not persist in doing shameful acts which only damage my relationship with other people and with Jesus.

January 6 – Feast of Epiphany and the Wise Men (Magi)

Do nothing from selfish ambition or conceit, but in humility regard others as better than yourselves.

Philippians 2:3

Reflection: Christian churches are open to everyone, even to those who do not accept the teachings of Jesus. There are no secret places in a Christian church and there are no secret rites. Christians are not allowed to have hidden agendas, or ulterior motives, and we are not to attempt to undermine people because of envy. If we regard others as better than we are, then we do not take them for granted and we are always prepared to respect their talents. As any student knows, it is better to imagine a very difficult test and be too prepared, than to be surprised by a difficult exam. When we study hard and prepare ourselves for an examination, then the actual test appears easy. From a moral point of view, if we regard other people as decent, then we are more likely to keep trying to be decent as well.

Prayer: Father, may I always approach life with humility and care, and may my actions always be motivated by goodwill towards other people.

January 7 - Christmas (Julian Calendar)

Satan, who is the god of this world, has blinded the minds of those who don't believe. They are unable to see the glorious light of the Good News. They don't understand this message about the glory of Christ, who is the exact likeness of God.

2 Corinthians 4:4

Reflection: It is quite understandable, that one might question the origin of life, or question books which claim to have the truth. But it is not satisfactory to assume that we know all there is to know about human origin. People who deny the existence of God become their own god and do as they please. Once we have decided on a sinful course of action, we begin to justify what we are about to do and we soon become blinded by the perceived rewards of sin. But the fact that we have to justify a behavior, is a good sign that we are about to do something sketchy. Like alcohol, wicked thoughts and wicked acts distort our perception of what is important and what is good. The purer the heart, the more clearly we perceive God. But that does not mean that atheists are any more wicked than non-atheists – many atheists have admirable attributes. However, it is difficult for anyone who is not willing to submit to the Spirit to understand God just as it is impossible for anyone who strives for a pure heart to be hostile to God.

Prayer: Lord, cleanse me of my faults so that I may perceive more clearly and so that my mind may clearly see You in all that You have created.

January 8

Let the words of my mouth and the meditation of my heart be acceptable to You, O Lord, my rock and my redeemer.

Psalm 19:14

Reflection: The mouth can be a source of goodness or of evil. And what we allow our heart to dwell on can also be positive or negative. The danger is not so much the words that we speak to God but the words that we speak to one another. Our words should help to build others and encourage them towards God and our meditations should be so pure that we should be willing to share them with other people. When we come to God, we must be prepared to acknowledge our faults. Sin is not just the visible wrongs we do to others; sin includes negative thoughts, envy, negative attitudes, and many of the things we do in secret. We are asked to put all these things on the table so that we might be cleansed, forgiven, and rebuilt afresh.

Prayer: Spirit of God, help me to feel secure, and may I not delight in the misfortune of other people or use words to hurt or abuse them.

January 9

Folly Calls for a Hearing. The woman named Folly is brash. She is ignorant and doesn't know it. She sits in her doorway on the heights overlooking the city. She calls out to men going by who are minding their own business. "Come in with me," she urges the simple. To those who lack good judgment, she says, "Stolen water is refreshing; food eaten in secret tastes the best!" But little do they know that the dead are there. Her guests are in the depths of the grave.

Proverbs 9:18

Reflection: The image conjured up by the verse above is that of a woman luring men to an illicit relationship with her. Men do the same thing. Sin is about the false promise of pleasure and the lack of good judgment. Disobedience separates us from God and, since it is God that sustains us, separation from God can mean suffering or even death. Sometimes we are beaten down spiritually by an accumulation of wickedness. Guilt which arises from wrongdoings weighs us down, sinks our conscience and weakens our body making us susceptible to diseases. The last thing we want as we pray to God in our hour of need is to have our conscience condemn us because of things we have not dealt with. We want God to make our life joyful and so we must strive to make life joyful for others. Selfish desires which make others weep will only eventually bring us sorrow and bodily pain. Wickedness is unsustainable.

Prayer: Thank You for giving me life, God. I pray that my life will be pleasing to You and that I might continue to be sustained by Your grace.

January 10

Brothers and sisters, do not slander one another. Anyone
who speaks against a brother or a sister, or judges them
speaks against the law and judges it. When you judge the
law, you are not keeping it, but sitting in judgment on it.

James 4:11

Reflection: No one likes to be the butt of other people's jokes, or to be
the subject of discussions behind one's back, regardless of whether the
joke or what is being talked about is true or false. Making up stories at
the expense of other people or spreading negative things about others
is slander and is harmful. Envy or jealousy is often the root of slander
and its main objective is to undermine another person. This is why
gossip or slander is wickedness and as this verse reminds us, to use
the colloquial phrase, what goes around, does indeed come around.

Prayer: Father, may I never delight in listening to gossip and may my
tongue and hands build up other people, rather than destroy their
characters.

Then He adds: "Their sins and lawless acts I will remember no more."

Hebrews 10:17

Reflection: Forgiveness is difficult for us because we conveniently forget our own faults. But God is all about forgiveness. We easily forget that this is God's world and that before we were born He had set the rules for human existence. And so the entire purpose of our life on earth is to bring us closer to God. His laws, as they relate to human behavior, awaken in us a sense of morality, and make us understand that it is only through learning to love each other that we are most content. And so when we repent and turn away from disobedience God extends forgiveness to us. We mature physically just by staying alive, but more is required from us if we wish to mature in spirit.

Prayer: Thank you, Father, for forgetting my sins. Help me to forget them as well and help me to pass on the forgiveness I have received from You to others.

January 12

But now you must also rid yourselves of all such things
as these: anger, rage, malice, slander, and filthy language
from your lips.

Colossians 3:8

Reflection: Lingering anger is a sign that there are people out there
that we don't wish well. But anger causes more harm to the person
feeling anger. People who are easily angered tend to have more health
issues and are less popular with their family and friends. God hears
prayers that come from the heart and it is impossible to pray for healing
in good faith when our heart is seeking revenge on people who offend
us. Healing our own wounds requires that we close open wounds with
other people. A wise person then is one who is always ready to extend
an olive branch to his adversaries.

Prayer: Spirit of God, please make me wise so that I do not respond
with anger whenever I disagree with people. Help me to realize that I
am happier when I refuse to let anger be a part of my day.

January 13

Jesus was still teaching when four people came up, carrying a crippled man on a mat. But because of the crowd, they could not get him to Jesus. So they made a hole in the roof above him and let the man down in front of everyone. When Jesus saw how much faith they had, he said to the crippled man, "My friend, your sins are forgiven."

Mark 2:5

Reflection: This is an interesting passage which gives us insight on the relationship between sin and suffering. In the remainder of the verse we learn that the man was healed after his sins were forgiven. If we believe in a loving all-powerful God, then it is understandable that we would consider physical pain as a sign that all is not well with us spiritually. After all God can make us well if God wishes. People in the Bible believed that sin was the cause of pain and suffering. At one point, when Christ was healing a blind man, His disciples even asked Jesus: "Who sinned, this man or his parents that he should be born blind?" However, Jesus told them that neither had sinned to cause the blindness. While it is true that sin provides a means for the devil to attack us physically, it does not follow that having physical disabilities or physical imperfections are a sign of unforgiven sin.

Prayer: Father God I pray for faith as strong as that of the crippled man. Help me to understand the source of suffering in my life.

January 14

<hr />

So do not fear, for I am with you; do not be dismayed, for I am your God. I will strengthen you and help you; I will uphold you with my righteous right hand.

Isaiah 41:10

Reflection: We fear because we imagine that bad things we have seen happen to others will happen to us and we fear when we ignore God's promise that we will never have to bear more than we can handle. God did not create us to endure torture or to watch us in anguish. Even when we make terrible mistakes which brings us trouble, God is still there with us. And so rather than allow fear to paralyze us or to rob us of hope, we should trust in God as we strive to grow in spiritual gifts and obedience. Those who have trusted God tell us that fear can bring us more pain than physical ailments do.

Prayer: Spirit of God, help me to not be so concerned with myself. Help me to relax and to trust in You, so that I will not let fear rob me of joy.

January 15

Furthermore, because we are united with Christ, we have received an inheritance from God, for He chose us in advance, and He makes everything work out according to His plan

Ephesians 1:11

Reflection: Though we might not understand all things in the world, we must have faith and we must believe that God has arranged for all things to lead us towards a better life. The family we are born into, the people we meet, the friends that we make, and every opportunity and even troubles that come our way – all these experiences are unique to us and are designed to help us address our individual shortcomings. Jesus taught us to pray that: "God's will be done on earth, as it is in heaven." We are God's highest and most valued creation, and God is determined that we will learn compassion, charity and forgiveness through the events and the people we encounter daily. Even when we reject God and persecute each other, God never gives up on us. Patiently, and with mercy, God's Spirit guides us forward to the truth.

Prayer: Father, thank You for Your everlasting love and Your kindness. May Your will come to pass in my life and may I learn life giving lessons from those You have put in my life.

January 16

Now faith is being sure of what we hope for and certain
of what we do not see.

Hebrews 11:1

Reflection: Two hundred years ago, scientists wondered what made milk and other food go bad. The Frenchman Pasteur said contamination from microorganisms was the culprit. But microscopes were yet to be fully developed and since the naked eye could not see bacteria, other scientists disagreed with Pasteur. In a famous experiment Pasteur proved that bacteria do exist. He thus demonstrated that what cannot be seen with the eye can nonetheless be shown to exist. Our faith is not wishful thinking just because we do not see God. The Christian faith is based on the experience and testimony of those who came before us and on our own experience. In fact faith does not demand that we suspend our sense of logic. Faith is about thinking good things after we have done the best we can, or after we have renounced our past transgressions. Faith grows by doing the things written in our hearts and then observing subsequent results. This is how we know that charity and love are better than hate and discrimination. And so if we become devoted through prayer to Jesus' teachings, our faith grows and, eventually, we begin to trust in the things that are beyond our understanding. Faith that originates from a loving heart does not lead us to do questionable or wicked things.

Prayer: Spirit of God, help me to be faithful to the things you have put in my heart, so that I may grow in faith. Help me to avoid pointless arguments on matters that are irrelevant, such as trying to understand how many angels can dance on a pinhead.

January 17

But if any strikes you on the right cheek, turn the other
also.

Matthew 5:39

Reflection: Christianity is about living a life pleasing to God and
about assisting others to come to God. Violence breeds more violence
while love brings more love. If we believe that it is okay to take an eye
for an eye, then we are free to strike back at those who strike us. The
problem is that in doing so, we are likely to escalate the situation.
A knife might come into play, maybe even a gun. Perhaps more
importantly, revenge does not allow our opponent to feel remorse.
On the other hand, if we refrain from retaliating, not only do we
diffuse the situation, but we are more likely to gain the respect of the
opponent and to cause him to reconsider. It is better to gain a new
friend than to maintain an enemy. Forgiveness is more appealing than
revenge. This is the wisdom that Jesus teaches.

Prayer: Lord, give me the strength to always walk away from a bad
situation. Help me to be strong enough to bear injuries without
seeking revenge.

January 18

---◦---

If you abide in Me, and My words abide in you, ask for
whatever you wish, and it will be done for you.

John 15:4

Reflection: With so much pain and suffering in the world, it is difficult to believe that all we have to do is follow the teachings of Jesus and all will be well in our world. What does it mean to abide in Jesus? It means that we are to read, study and meditate on His teachings daily and that we are to be constantly open to the teachings of the Holy Spirit. As Christians there will be days when we do not feel like praying and there will be rough times, but if we abide in Jesus we will emerge triumphant. Our existence is a journey designed to grow faith, wisdom, and love in us. Jesus, the Good Shepherd, guides us through perilous roadways. What we pray for may not happen instantly. But we know that if we persist, it will happen a lot quicker than we imagine.

Prayer: Lord, help me to abide in the straight and narrow way which leads to sustained peace and joy and give me the patience to remain on the road even if it is long and hard.

January 19

He has blinded their eyes and hardened their heart, so
that they might not look with their eyes, and understand
with their heart, and turn, and I would heal them.

John 12:40

Reflection: We are not expected to read these words in a strict literal
sense; rather they are written to illustrate a point. God does not blind
eyes or harden people's hearts. Human wickedness distorts our eyes,
and hardens our hearts, and causes people to argue about the reality of
God. However one of the things that sets humans apart from animals
is that we are spiritual beings, we have a conscience and so we know
the nature and consequences of our behavior. We know that we affect
others by what we do and that we can also affect our physical health
by our behavior. Wickedness degrades the body, clouds the mind,
and robs us of faith. When we abide in the teachings of Jesus we gain
faith. Without faith, we have no hope and we are unable to believe in
a loving God. Because God hears every prayer from the heart, people
with hardened hearts are unable to turn to God.

Prayer: Spirit of God, help me to remove the things which cloud
my understanding. Help me to do away with rationalization of my
shortcomings so that I may confront my weaknesses and learn from
them.

January 20

Put on the armor that God gives, so that you can defend yourself against the devil's tricks.

Ephesians 6:11

Reflection: No one knows what is around the corner. Jesus tells us however that we should not worry about things that are outside of our control. A wise person cherishes the counsel of the Lord and seeks the help that only the Holy Spirit can offer. Prayer is the best medicine for daily living. It is not that God will not protect us unless we pray, it is that prayer helps us understand our weaknesses and strengths, and helps us understand how we may have strayed from the path of the Lord. If evil was presented to us in a straightforward manner we would all reject it. But evil often comes sugar-coated. Prayer helps us to see evil for what it is, and prayer helps us to focus our energy on the right things.

Prayer: Father God, I often find myself too lazy to pray, especially when things are going well in my life. Help me to cultivate a prayer life so that daily, I might wear the armor that will lead me not into temptation but deliver me from evil.

January 21

---◦◦◦---

*If any want to become My followers, let them deny
themselves and take up their cross and follow Me.*

Matthew 16:24

Reflection: Jesus is asking us to deny the animal drives and impulses
we have and to concentrate on spiritual pursuits. But why do we have
an animal nature in the first case if we are to reject it? The answer
is that we need a body to function in our physical world, but the
body we wear, like any animal body, is designed to survive through
brute force and guile. To survive and reproduce, animals must be fit,
and adaptable to the environment. On the other hand the spirit in
us thrives only on love and is quietened by any form of violence or
selfish deceit. Through this interaction between our animal nature
and spiritual awareness, we perfect the free will of love. Jesus gave
up a human existence in order to serve our needs. Jesus then is the
spiritual teacher, we are the students. To deny oneself is to follow in
the footsteps of Jesus.

Prayer: Spirit of God, help me to be attentive and eager to serve just
like my Master, Jesus. Help me to value decency and goodness over
animal pleasures which are at the expense of other people.

January 22

Fulfill what you vow.

Ecclesiastes 5:4

Reflection: When we make a promise, we should know that other people rely on the promise, and that they will draw conclusions regarding our character based on whether we fulfill the promise. Doing favors for other people or keeping the promises we make, may sometimes involve inconvenience for us. But unless circumstances have changed drastically, it is noble to keep promises. But circumstances do change and so if we can't fulfill our promise, we must let the other person know immediately. Anything short of this creates unease and mistrust. We are not to take promises lightly. True spiritual faith is about integrity.

Prayer: Lord, give me wisdom so that I will always consider my options before I make promises, and help to always fulfill what I promised.

January 23

Happy are those who do not follow the advice of the wicked, or take the path that sinners tread.

Psalm 1:1

Reflection: A bad advice we often receive from others goes: "Follow your heart for you only have one life to live." This type of advice is another way of telling us to ignore what our conscience is telling us and to do what will bring us pleasure. The advice of the wicked is that whatever brings us pleasure is okay. However, Jesus said, "By their fruits, you shall know them". So before we start taking advice from others on how to live, it is wise to consider the source of the advice. We should take advice from people who reflect the values that we aspire to. The Spirit speaks to us from inside and never leads us astray. And the teachings of Jesus are very clear and sufficient to guide us to the truth.

Prayer: Spirit of God, may I always be receptive to Your voice and to Your voice alone so that I may reject short-term pleasures, which are at the expense of my long-term happiness, and the happiness of my family.

January 24

———◦◦◦———

This people honor Me with their lips, but their hearts are far from Me; in vain they worship Me, teaching human precepts as doctrines. You abandon the commandments of God and hold on to human tradition.

Mark 7: 6-8

Reflection: Cults are often about traditions and secrecy. The leaders of cults teach very rigid rules and they discourage their followers from associating with non-cult members. In cults, traditions and rules are more important than people. Cults do not welcome scrutiny or open debates about their practices. Cults have traditions that do not make any sense or serve good purposes. Unlike Christian churches which are always open, cults have secrets, or hidden agendas that they do not wish to share with the public. Jesus was often found in the midst of the poor, the sick, and the downtrodden. In so doing, Jesus showed that our Father is there with everyone in need, regardless of their tribal origin or faith background. The story told by Jesus, of the Good Samaritan reminds us that people are more important than traditions.

Prayer: Spirit of God, help me to do first those things that reflect love and compassion for others. And help me to do away with human traditions that separate people from one another.

January 25

Daughter, your faith has made you well; go in peace and be healed of your disease.

Mark 5:43

Reflection: Faith is one of the highest gifts from God. With faith, all things are possible. Faith enables us to harness the spiritual power within us. Jesus didn't come with fanfare and glitter; He didn't even come from a priestly family and, as a result, many of the religious leaders scorned Him. But there were people, such as this woman in the verse above, who had followed Him around and formed her own opinion based on what she witnessed. This woman had seen enough to know that Jesus was special even if the religious leaders rejected Him. Her faith enabled her to turn to Jesus and to be cured.

Prayer: Holy Spirit of God, grant me the faith to put my hope and trust in the kindness of the Lord and to be able to see the wonders of God through my eyes.

January 26

But I say to you, love your enemies and pray for those who persecute you so that you may be children of your Father in heaven.

Matthew 5:44-45

Reflection: In many parts of the world, people are taught that they have enemies who wish to kill them and that they must be ready to fight to protect what is dear to them. However, Jesus Christ has a very different opinion when it comes to human relationships especially when we are interacting with people with whom we have differences. In fact, one of the things that sets Jesus apart from everyone else is his insistence that we are to pray for our enemies and that we should love people who do not like us. Without the Spirit to help us understand it, this teaching seems like foolishness and is rarely practiced. This is why there is always a war going on somewhere in the world and why so many countries in the world are purveyors of deadly weapons.

Prayer: Father, I thank You for forgiving my wrongdoings. Help me to put myself in the shoes of my adversaries so that I can empathize with their cause, and treat them with kindness and love.

January 27

Fight the good fight of the faith.

1 Timothy 6:12

Reflection: To fight the good fight is to live according to the teachings of the Lord. When we do so, we win over doubters. Without faith, we soon decide that it does not matter whether we do good or bad. We become our own god, creating our own rules, and doing as we please. When we do this, we live like lower animals. But because we have the capability to do better, our choices have mental significances. Bad choices bring mental anguish. The good fight of faith is what enables us to put aside the cravings of the flesh in the belief that a spiritual life will bring us greater and lasting peace and happiness.

Prayer: Father, I desire to do good and I know that my faith carries me beyond where my intellect cannot go. Help me to fight the good fight daily. Today I will practice my faith by casting my worries unto the Lord.

January 28

Those who guard their mouths and their tongues keep themselves from calamity.

Proverbs 21:23

Reflection: We sometimes wish that we could take back something that we have said. Sadly our tongue is not always under our control. Who can say that she has never said unkind things to other people? Careless talk is a blunder because sooner or later, we come to realize that it brings us nothing but pain or misery. If we would not repeat a gossip in the presence of the subject, then this is a good indication that we should hold our tongue. A Christian tongue should only be used in good faith. God cares about what we say about other people, as this verse illustrates.

Prayer: Father, help me to always remember that I cannot take back what I say. I pray that I may always be more eager to listen than to speak.

January 29

Why are you afraid, you of little faith?

Matthew 8:26

Reflection: We are afraid because we fear the unknown and we want control over everything that affects our life. We have a wish list for how life should be and anything that appears to jeopardize our wish list, or our desire, creates fear. We all know people who appear to be doomed by an illness and we shudder at the thought that we could share their fate. The fact is that, yes, we go through hard times, but the chances are, if we look back at life, we will discover that the biggest source of pain is fear itself. Actual problems never last; they pass and we adjust. Holding on to faith helps us to focus on the important things in life and to ignore other things. Our faith of course grows by practicing what the Lord teaches. In this passage, Jesus is asking us to remember that even when we don't have control, God does.

Prayer: Spirit of God, strengthen my faith daily and help me to become a good example of steadfast faith for my family and friends.

January 30

Train a child in the way he should go, and when he is old,
he will not turn from it.

Proverbs 22:6

Reflection: One of our biggest responsibilities is offering guidance and assistance to our children. Unfortunately, many of us did not have the best family situation and so we often lack the skills to pass on many good habits and knowledge. Providentially, we have a perfect Father in God and, if we pay attention, we soon realize that God is the best teacher possible. And so the best teaching we can pass on to our children is curiosity about God and about creation. But we should refrain from forcing our beliefs on our children. Jesus never forced anyone and he has not asked us to force others into the faith.

Prayer: Lord, help me to tell the difference between passing on dogmas to my children and fueling their curiosity on the meaning of life. May I always be a good influence on my children's spiritual growth.

January 31

For God did not give us a spirit of timidity but a spirit of power, of love, and of self-discipline.

2 Timothy 1:7

Reflection: According to tradition, all but one of the Apostles of Jesus were put to death on account of their faith; some died locally, while others were martyred as far away as India. We thank God today that they each had the strength and power to hang on to their faith even when their lives were at stake. Those who put them to death probably wondered where their superhuman power to keep their faith in the face of death, came from. Only God knows how many countless number of people came to embrace the teachings of Jesus, after witnessing the faith of the Apostles. This is the work of the Holy Spirit. While it may not seem that way to us at times, we are made in the image of God and, through Christ, we have been adopted into God's family. Jesus, over and over, reminded the disciples that humans are special to God and that we have great powers. Peter was able to walk on water until he became afraid. Rather than fear, we need to learn self-discipline and self-respect.

Prayer: Lord, teach me to respect others and help me to be bold, fearless, and loving in my interactions with other people.

February 1

---◦◦---

Those who belong to Christ Jesus have crucified the flesh with its passions and desires.

Galatians 5:24

Reflection: To be human is to have the physical capacity to experience passion like animals do. We all know the power of a raging bull and who can blame a bull for being a bull. But humans have two things that bulls do not have: First, we can appreciate the consequences of our actions; and second, we have free will to choose what we do. So unlike a bull, we are not blameless if we let passion control us. Our responsibility is to live a life that is harmless and pleasing to God. The glory of the bull is his brute force. The glory of a person is self-control.

Prayer: Lord, may I always reflect Your glory rather than live as a raging bull, and be gripped by destructive passions.

February 2

---

*It is easier for a camel to go through the eye of a needle
than for a rich person to enter the kingdom of God.*

Mark 10:25

Reflection: Many of us dream of making a lot more money than we currently do, or we wish we were born with a silver spoon. But the truth is that we are all rich. There is always someone with less money than we have and everyone has the capacity to give love, and to spread joy to others. The monthly wage of a laborer in Alberta, is considered a fortune in South Sudan. In short, we are all rich where it counts. We all have the capacity to serve each other. So whether it is a timely visit, a phone call or a loan of money, we are called to be our brother's keeper and to use the gifts that God entrusts to us with love. Jesus tells us that if we use what little we have wisely, we can expect to be entrusted with more from God. And so those who refuse to make their gifts available for the good of others are in danger of straying from the teachings of Jesus.

Prayer: Spirit of God, direct me to those who need my aid, and help me to understand that it is better for me to give than to receive.

February 3

If you do not doubt in your heart, but believe that what you say will come to pass, it will be done for you.

Mark 11:23-24

Reflection: This simple verse from Jesus speaks to what it means to be human; we are spirits confined in a physical body. The spirit within us can do anything and is not bound by the laws of physics. But there is only one way to harness this spiritual power – through obedience to God. If we are obedient God grants us unwavering faith that can move mountains. Obedience brings understanding; understanding brings faith and faith does miracles. As well, obedience brings perfect love which in turn drives out fear. And so a person with no love in his heart is always in doubt and cannot be an instrument for performing miracles.

Prayer: Holy Spirit of God, help me to become obedient to God like my Lord and Savior. Help me to harness the spiritual power within me for the benefit of the Kingdom.

February 4

*You, O Lord, are a shield around me, my glory, and the
One who lifts up my head.*

Psalm 3:3

Reflection: A woman once said to God: "Lord, I am sorry that the world is full of problems; there are so many people in pain. Lord, You do not have to worry about me any longer, I will look after myself from now on so You can spend more time helping other people." These words were said in good faith, but within moments after they were uttered, everything began to go wrong for that person. The change was so sudden and dramatic that she was convinced that she was having a psychotic experience. The crisis only came to an end after she retracted what she had said to God. This story illustrates how little we appreciate the fact that it is God that sustains us. Indeed if we have any splendor, or if people have any regard for us, it is because of the safeguards that God has around us.

Prayer: Spirit of God, I know that I was a dejected person until You came and lifted up my head. Your glory shines on me. I thank You for all that You do to sustain me.

February 5

Religion that is pure and undefiled before God, the Father, is this: to care for orphans and to keep oneself unstained by the world.

James 1:27

Reflection: We have made a mess of life on earth. All the countries in the world spend more money on guns and weapons than they do caring for vulnerable people in their midst. One irony here is that it is often these weapons that create orphans and widows. Religion is not about judging others or about figuring out who is or who is not destined for heaven or for hell. Judgment is God's domain. Our domain is to spread love and joy and to bear the burden of those less fortunate amongst us. Children of God are at the forefront of peace, not war, at the forefront of love, not revenge; Christians are to be at the forefront of charity, and not discrimination.

Prayer: Father, may I reflect Your attributes to all those that I come across. Help me to be there for those who need my assistance.

February 6

———⋙◦⋘———

*Be sure to fear the Lord and serve Him faithfully with
all your heart; consider what great things He has done
for you.*

First Book of Samuel 12:24

Reflection: People who count their blessings are happier than those
who dwell on what they are missing. We would not cease counting
if we were to number all the blessings we have received from God.
Nonetheless it is a good idea to stop and to reflect on our blessings
from time to time. If we are honest we would admit that we don't
deserve much of what we have. It is God that covers our transgressions
and it is God that blesses the work of our hands. Jesus once healed
ten lepers but only one came back to give thanks. We want to be that
person who gives thanks to God.

Prayer: Father, I know lots of people who work harder and are more
skilled than I am. Thank You for giving me so much more than I
deserve and thank You that I can always count on Your love. Today I
will remember how good God has been to me.

February 7

As for me, I am in Your hands; do with me whatever You think is good and right.

Jeremiah 26:14

Reflection: This is the ultimate desire: to unconditionally give back our will to God. But giving back our will involves a continuous giving affirmation that is reflected in all that we think and do. It is a difficult thing to give oneself unconditionally because we fear the unknown. But we can be assured that God will not bring us misery when we turn to Him.

Prayer: Spirit of God, help me to let go so that my will and desire will always be to walk behind my Master Jesus. Today I will do what my Lord wants me to do.

February 8

Delight yourself also in the Lord: and He shall give you the desires of your heart.

Psalm 37:4-5

Reflection: If God is able and wanting to give us all the good desires of our heart, then what is stopping God from doing so? The answer is that we stand in the way. In fact, if God were satisfied that riches would draw us closer to Him and not hinder our spiritual growth, then we would have all the riches that we ask for. The reason that it sometimes takes a while to "answer" our prayer is that prayers involve the type of spiritual awakenings that come through experience. Jesus said that we are capable of moving mountains and so God often uses our prayers to help us realize that power. If we seek first the Kingdom of God (love, diligence, and compassion, etc.), everything else shall be added unto us. So whatever we ask for that poses no issue for others, we shall have so long as we are willing to learn how to handle the gifts from God.

Prayer: Lord, fill me with a desire for You so that my days and nights shall be in adoration of You. Today I will delight in God.

February 9

This is what the Lord says: "Let not the wise boast of their wisdom or the strong boast of their strength or the rich boast of their riches, but let the one who boasts boast about this: that they have the understanding to know Me, that I am the Lord, who exercises kindness, justice and righteousness on earth for in these I delight," declares the Lord.

Jeremiah 9:23-24

Reflection: To know the Lord is to turn our mind away from harmful pursuits and to follow in the steps of Jesus. God is found all around us and so if we do everything for God's glory, then we will gain in understanding, life will yield many more secrets and joy. We come into life with nothing and so we have nothing to boast about. We are allowed one boast: that we love God and His Christ.

Prayer: Father, simple things, like cleaning up after myself, taking my work seriously, watching only appropriate shows on television, and refusing to surf the internet aimlessly, reflect my love and desire for You. May what I do or think today never cause the Holy Spirit to flee from me.

February 10

Rabbi, we know that you are a teacher who has come from God. For no one could perform the signs you are doing if God were not with him.

John 3:2

Reflection: Many people who witnessed the miracles that Jesus performed were convinced that Jesus was from God. Aside from his disciples Jesus had many other followers who were afraid to profess their faith openly. Nicodemus was one such man. He was a leader in his community and he came to Jesus at night to profess his faith in Jesus. If Nicodemus was alive today he would say that only God could have made the teachings of a man who was crucified as an outlaw captivate people around the world. Indeed many historians believe that modern civilization was made possible by the teachings of Jesus. It is self-evident that only God could have brought about the miracles we read in the Gospels.

Prayer: Lord Jesus, we have not seen You in person and we cannot see the Father but we believe You are from the Father because our hearts tell us that Your teachings are perfect as only God can be perfect. Today I will boast of my delight in Your teachings.

February 11

Obedience to God comes before obedience to men.

Acts 5:29

Reflection: Peter and the other Apostles of Jesus had been warned by the authorities not to teach about Jesus in Jerusalem. They went against this order and when they were apprehended, the above verse was their response to the authorities. Religious persecution is still with us. Christian churches had been guilty, as were other faiths in persecuting those they disagree with. Today there are places in the world where people are not allowed to follow their religious conscience. And even in countries where there is religious freedom, there are still groups that exert pressure on members of their community, so that they do not follow their conscience. And then there are people who spread violence and terror, ostensibly in the name of their God. Anyone that knows God will attest that God will never ask us to hurt other people or to spread terror. God is love and so actions that do not reflect love are not of God.

Prayer: Father God, I know that all good things come from You. I pray that I may never allow myself to fall into a situation where I am spreading false teachings. Today, I will not entertain violence in my thoughts and in my words.

February 12

But let none of you suffer as a murderer or a thief or an evil doer or as a meddler.

1 Peter 4:15

Reflection: This passage seems to consider meddling in the same light as murder. A meddler is a person who injects himself into other people's disagreements. Meddlers fuel disagreements rather than promote peace and harmony. We see this every day in the wars around the world. Sometimes one country is supplying arms to both sides of a dispute. Without meddlers, many of the wars in the world will die out. No wonder the Bible is so contemptuous of meddlers.

Prayer: Holy Spirit, a child of God does not meddle in other people's affairs, except to promote love and peace. Help me to sow love where there is hate so that both sides of a dispute might seek reconciliation.

February 13

And without faith, it is impossible to please Him, for whoever would draw near to God must believe that He exists and that He rewards those who seek Him.

Hebrews 11:6

Reflection: Paul's reasoning in this letter to Hebrew followers of Jesus appears to be circular. The question is how do we know that God exists, so we can then draw close to God and have faith in Him. There is enough evidence in the world even outside of history or Scripture to make any skeptic wonder about human origin. Even scientists who believe in the theory of evolution see patterns in nature which suggest the existence of a power outside of human perception. Moreover in every culture in the world, there exists the idea of a Creator. But there is one thing that we cannot avoid: the small voice inside us which tries to direct our path. We can quibble about the origin of conscience but there is no mistaking the voice of conscience when we are about to do wrong. For those who demand proof of God's existence, this is a place to start – anyone who resolves to live in accordance with their conscience can see whether or not in so doing a path for perceiving God opens up.

Prayer: Father I know that the growth of my faith depends on doing the things I already know in my conscience. Today help me to live my faith.

February 14

*Two are better than one, because they have a good reward
for their toil. For if they fall, one will lift up the other.*

Ecclesiastes 4:9

Reflection: The Bible tells us that after God created Adam, God then
created Eve so that Adam would not be alone. In countries founded on
Christian principles monogamy is normal (although in actual present-
day practice, it is more accurate to speak of serial monogamy). Humans
crave companionship, and studies show that children brought up by
parents living together fare better than other children. People living as
couples have higher disposable incomes, live longer and are healthier,
than single people. As divorce rates rise we see more social problems
with children from broken homes. God is no longer allowed to play
a major role in the lives of many people, and so the sacrament of
marriage and the marriage oath, are becoming meaningless to them.
Christian teaching however has not changed. We know that growing
old in the arms of the spouse of our youth is a blessing worth striving
for. [It is no coincidence that this passage comes on the Feast Day of
St. Valentine, in which the love between spouses is celebrated in some
Church traditions and in popular culture.]

Prayer: Spirit of God, help me to be faithful to my spouse in my
thoughts, in my words, in what I do, and in what I fail to do. Help me
to appreciate my family and to not take my spouse for granted.

February 15

You will know them by their fruits. Are grapes gathered
from thorns, or figs from thistles?

Matthew 7:16

Reflection: It is easy to make claims about God and about having
found favor in the hands of God. But as the song goes: "By our love
they will know we are Christians." Unfortunately we sometimes fail
God by how we treat each other or by the claims we make about God.
In the news recently was the story of a child who was forced to fast by
his parents because it was thought that he was possessed by the devil.
The child was two years old and his parents were Christian pastors.
The little boy died of starvation. A terrible thing. This type of thing
happens when we try to tell God what to do rather than listen to God.
Jesus is the revelation of God and Jesus alone perfectly reflects the
attributes of God. And so we are to be skeptical of claims not rooted
in love and in forgiveness. The fruit of God's vine is love of all, nothing
else. Medicine and the physicians who practice medicine are blessed
by God, as are those who preach the Gospel in our churches.

Prayer: Lord, may those I meet see in me Your fruits, that they too
may seek to work in Your vineyard. Thank You, that You have enabled
us to understand so much about the human body and about our
environment. Today I will bless physicians who seek to heal the sick.

February 16

I am the good shepherd. The good shepherd lays down his life for the sheep.

John 10:11

Reflection: Domesticated sheep hardly know where the best pasture is or where the next danger is lurking. They depend on the shepherd for everything. And so we too, as spiritual beings, depend on the Holy Spirit sent to us by Jesus. On our own, we only mess things up and end up as prey for evil schemers.

Prayer: Jesus, please keep me in Your fold and deliver me from every evil and from wolves that seek to devour me.

February 17

My dear brothers and sisters, take note of this: Everyone should be quick to listen, slow to speak and slow to become angry.

James 1:19

Reflection: The fact that we have two ears, and one mouth suggests that we are to listen twice as much as we speak. No two people see or feel life exactly the same way. So there is something to be learned from everyone we encounter and if we cultivate a habit of good listening and reflection, we will learn a lot. Much of the answers to our spiritual and other questions, are out there, and as the Holy Spirit clears the fog created by sin and disobedience, we will understand a lot more about the forces that shape us.

Prayer: Spirit of God, please help me to become a calm and attentive person and help me to respect others, no matter how different their opinions are from mine.

February 18

Let the little children come to me and do not stop them; for it is to such as these that the kingdom of heaven belongs.

Matthew 19:13

Reflection: Little children have innocence and the desire to learn. Children were special to Jesus because they were blameless. Little children can be mischievous and do things that are hurtful, but because they have not developed full appreciation for what it means to put oneself in the shoes of another, they are innocent from a moral point of view. Normal adults do have this appreciation and so there is blame for acting in bad faith. Jesus calls adults to become like children because the message of God, seen by an uncorrupted mind, is compelling. It is true as well that even when we become adults, our relationship with God remains that of child/parent in that it is God's energy that continues to sustain us.

Prayer: Spirit of God, purify my heart so that I may live simply as You intended me to live and so that I may not complicate the simple truths that Jesus taught.

February 19

Let us love, not in word or speech but in truth and action.

1 John 3:18

Reflection: Talk is cheap. We can stand on the highest pulpit and proclaim our love for each other, but who would believe us unless this love is put into action? What better way to witness God's love to others than to be there for them, helping and assisting with joy? It is easy to claim that we are children of God but the evidence has to come from our choices. If we remind others of God by how we treat them, we will draw them to God. If, on the other hand, there is only speech, and empty claims, what good does that do? Many Japanese people upon witnessing mercy from Americans at the end of World War II, converted to Christianity (use of the atomic bomb, notwithstanding). The people and countries most admired in the world adhere to Christian principles, even when they profess no faith.

Prayer: Father, I pray that I will put as much effort into cleansing my heart and my thoughts as I put into cleaning up my outward behavior.

February 20

These are also sayings of the wise. Partiality in judging is not good.

John 7:24

Reflection: One of the most hurtful things we can do is to pass judgment on people for things that are beyond their control. When we laugh at someone because of their looks we are laughing at their Maker. Did you know that we tend to be kinder to nicer looking people? Psychologists found that parents who were shown pictures of school children selected the nicer looking kids as less troublesome. Skin color sometimes works the same way in that we tend to be partial to people who look like us. If we are to treat others as we would like to be treated then we have to be careful that we don't make people feel bad based on the basis of their outward appearance. People have a common origin.

Prayer: Spirit of God, teach me to love and to respect all that I come across. Remind me always that we are all children of God with equal but different gifts.

February 21

---

*Lift your drooping shoulders and strengthen your weak
knees and make straight paths for your feet.*

Hebrews 12:12

Reflection: Active people are usually strong and fit. The more we
move around the happier our body is. No one ever finds lasting joy by
being slack. People who take their work seriously find so much joy in
doing their best. We have each been provided with unique tools and
with talents with which to contribute to the world. It is therefore a sign
of ingratitude to waste time and to waste our abilities. There is always
someone who could use our help. Droopy shoulders and weak knees
can be made strong again by volunteering our time for the benefit of
others.

Prayer: Spirit of God, prepare me daily so that I may always do my
best and, in so doing, be a good role model for my family. Help me to
rise with enthusiasm each morning.

February 22

Better is open rebuke than love that is concealed. Faithful are the wounds of a friend, but deceitful are the kisses of an enemy.

Proverbs 27:5-6

Reflection: Friends and strangers are often pivotal in terms of how successful we are in life. When we treat people well, they wish us well and they want us around and they will invite us into friendships and business ventures. The particular combination of friends we have is exactly what we require to complement our personality. This is part of God's plan. Some friends will teach us patience by challenging us. Others will teach us kindness because they will require our help. Learning to appreciate our friends is a way to thank the Lord for bringing them into our life.

Prayer: Father, thank you for my friends. Help me to appreciate them and help me to be there for them. Today I will take time to appreciate my friends.

February 23

Is a lamp brought in to be under the bushel basket, or under the bed and not on the lampstand? For there is nothing hidden except to be disclosed; nor is anything secret except to come to light.

Mark 4:21

Reflection: Jesus called his disciples to teach them the way of God so they can preach the Good News to the world. Every person that is redeemed by God is called to become a testimony to the world. The Holy Spirit works through us. And so, as we grow in wisdom and faith, God wants us to reflect on the things we have learned from others. If we have received mercy, let us pass mercy on. If we have wisdom, let us pass it on. If we have faith, let us live it. Many of us were rejected by the world, as nobodies, but through Christ we have become lamps for the world.

Prayer: Spirit of God, may Your light shine brightly in me so that I may glow for those who are still in darkness. Today I will let my actions witness my gratitude to Jesus.

February 24

For everyone will be salted with fire.

Mark 9:49

Reflection: Salt is what ancient people used to preserve food, salt keeps food from spoiling. Fire is painful, but pain often causes us to re-evaluate our perspectives on life and it teaches us not to take life for granted. The conflicts in our lives, the troubles we encounter, are two means of finding out who we are and what we are lacking. Self-knowledge is required for growth and, as we overcome obstacles, we learn about ourselves. In fact, when there are no trials and tribulations in our lives, we are usually not growing. Since the Lord's goal for us is a pure heart and pure thoughts, all of the frustration we experience daily show us what we need to overcome. The more we experience frustrations, the more we know we are growing. Those who are salted with fire are those who have been prepared for discipleship.

Prayer: Father God, thank You for counting me worthy to be salted and made ready to withstand the trials and tribulations that come with carrying my cross daily. May the Holy Spirit grant me the strength and fortitude to remain diligent and faithful in whatever my hands find to do.

February 25

Love must be sincere. Hate what is evil; cling to what is good

Romans 12:9

Reflection: No one who loves God can hate his brothers and sisters. No one who loves God can bring violence and hate to other people. Many claims are made in the name of God. Christians are often accused of using and taking verses out of context in the Bible to justify sketchy actions specifically rejected by Jesus. Even wars and genocides have been done, supposedly in the name of God. We have all read about the Crusades and the atrocities alleged to have been carried out in the name of Jesus (as well as those carried out by other faiths). Extreme views, racism, and intolerance of people who are different have all been carried out in the name of God. This is why Jesus emphasized to His disciples that not all who claim to know Him actually do. To know Jesus is to renounce violence and all forms of wickedness. We are to test the spirit of all those who come to us in the name of the Lord. Jesus taught love and peace and so we must do the same thing.

Prayer: Spirit of God, search my heart and replace all hate or ill will towards others with love so that I might be worthy to serve in Your vineyard.

February 26

They tie up heavy burdens, hard to bear, and lay them on people's shoulders, but they themselves are not willing to move them with their finger.

Matthew 23:4

Reflection: Jesus reserved his sharpest criticism for the religious leaders of his day. Jesus had no patience for people who did not attempt to practice what they preached. Unfortunately we have all read about people who have used Jesus' name to amass wealth, or who have brought shame to themselves. Jesus in this passage is talking about leaders who try to use the Word of God to control other people. Followers of Jesus lead by example, they are humble servants of the people, not bullies or indoctrinators.

Prayer: Father, thank You for the servants You send to minister to the poor and to those without a voice. I pray that I never bring shame to Your church. Today I will not condemn other people for failing to do what I myself have failed to do.

February 27

In everything, do to others as you would have them do to you; for this is the law and the prophets.

Matthew 7:12

Reflection: Everyone appreciates a timely act of kindness or forgiveness. If we were alone in the world, then we could do as we please without offending anyone. But we share the earth with brothers and sisters and sometimes we may have an advantage that they don't have. Or we may have knowledge which enables us to take advantage of others. Ancient Egyptians took advantage of their number and took the Israelites as slaves. If we treated everyone in good faith, there would not be anyone who is hungry or cold.

Prayer: Spirit of God, help me to always remember not to take advantage of other people's weakness. Help me to treat others as I would wish to be treated.

February 28

Lazy people should learn a lesson from the way ants live.

Proverbs 6:6

Reflection: If you studied the habits of people you admire or respect you will find that these people usually live disciplined lives and that they value what they do with their time. People we admire are usually hard working. But hard work does not mean that we shouldn't enjoy life. On the contrary the harder we work the greater the capacity to enjoy and to be happy. Structure is the most important aspect of hard work because with structure we know when to rest and relax and our work will not spill over into play and we will not feel guilt while we play. We live in an imperfect world and as Christians we know that the work of creation continues. We also know that we have the ability to make the world a better place and to contribute to the world. What we do with time therefore becomes a moral issue. Aristotle said that happiness or Eudaimonia, is a life lived according to virtue. Hard work is a virtue.

Prayer: Father, I have seen that the more organised my life is the happier I am. Help me daily to make the best use of my time.

February 29

As crowds were gathering around Jesus, he said: "You people of today are evil! You keep looking for a sign from God."

Luke 11:29

Reflection: The people Jesus was speaking to flouted their conscience and lived as they pleased they seemed prepared to change their behavior only if Jesus showed them God. These people were not interested in goodness, but would follow Jesus only through fear. Jesus is speaking to us all, for the truth is that it is only when we begin to devote time to spiritual endeavours that we begin to covet goodness for its own sake. The fear of God should make us examine who we are but love for each other should make us strive to do unto others as we wish others would do unto us.

Prayer: Father, my faith comes from doing the things which I know to be good. Help me to look for You in the people that I meet and through the practice of Your son's teachings.

March 1

Do you think that because these Galileans suffered in this way they were worse sinners than all other Galileans? No, I tell you, but unless you repent, you will all perish as they did.

Luke 13:2-3

Reflection: Sometimes we are faced with situations where a beloved person is suffering. The question that often arises is whether we believe that a person who is ill is a worse sinner than other people. This verse by Jesus suggests that people do not always suffer because they are sinners. We have all sinned and so it is by the Grace of God that we are sustained. Why one sinner suffers and another seems to escape is a mystery. What is clear is that we are all called to repent, to shun wickedness in all its forms, and to become committed to spiritual growth. The lesson to take away from this verse is that sinning is a serious business.

Prayer: Come oh Spirit, and help me to forgive myself so that I may accept the Grace of God. Help me to show my love for Jesus by respecting the laws of his Father.

March 2

A friend loves at all times, and a brother is born for adversity.

Proverbs 17:17

Reflection: On the way to a job interview a man stopped to change a flat tire for a stranded woman on the highway. It turned out the woman was his potential employer he was going to meet. Friends and brothers are most valued in times of trouble. This is why we are reminded by God to cultivate goodness not just in those around us but in everyone we meet. Adversity helps us to understand how to respond to others in trouble and it helps us to appreciate the kindness of our friends. Our friends need us at all times, but more so in difficult times, when, without us, they may stand alone. Just before Jesus was handed over to the authorities, he spent time praying with his brethren. Our load is lighter when those around us lend a hand.

Prayer: Lord, teach me to be faithful to and to appreciate my friends and family, both in good times and in bad times.

March 3

It is better to hear the rebuke of the wise than to hear the songs of the fools.

Ecclesiastes 7:5

Reflection: Wise people offer advice out of love and they care about our welfare. When a wise person sees that we are creating trouble, he or she will not hesitate to let us know. But we often enjoy flattery. We like to listen to people who agree with us. However the verse above tells us that it is more useful for us to pay attention to criticism from people who love us and who wish us well. It is also a good idea to consider the source of any advice we receive. "By their fruits, you shall know them." When we heed the advice of a wise person we are liable to avoid headaches.

Prayer: Spirit of God, open my eyes so that I may see clearly the difference between empty flattery and a loving rebuke. Help me to appreciate the words of wise people around me.

March 4

And lead us not into temptation but deliver us from evil.
Matthew 6:13

Reflection: Visiting sketchy places or hanging out with trouble makers, is inviting trouble. Children growing up yearn for independence from their parents. And so we too normally try to live independently of God, the Father. Little do we know that we are actually on "life support". Everyone has so much sin, that if it wasn't for the grace of God, we would collapse under the weight of sin. Like a virus, sin self-multiplies under the direction of Satan and destroys its host. Our flesh can be ravaged by sin and weakened so badly by wickedness that we have little willpower on our own to resist evil. Sin is passed on from person to person and is irresistible without the Holy Spirit. And so it is important to watch where we go and whom we spend time with, so that we are not led into temptation. A wise person starts and ends each day with a prayer.

Prayer: Spirit of God, help me to always acknowledge how much I need and depend on You to keep me from giving in to temptation. I pray that I am always surrounded by people who are good influences.

March 5

But because of his great love for us, God who is rich in mercy, made us alive with Christ even when we were dead in transgressions-it is by grace you have been saved.

Ephesians 2:4:5

Reflection: If only we know how deep God's love is for us, we would better appreciate how ungrateful we are. It is God that calls people like Mother Teresa and Elizabeth Fry to minister to people most of us would rather forget. It is out of love that God calls people to visit the forgotten in prisons and to assist their families. Prisoners are people who have broken our laws and who have brought pain and shame to their families, to themselves, and to their victims. Yet God never forgets them. The desire and mission to be there for each other comes from God who is our strength.

Prayer: Father, I am often teary-eyed when I see how much You love people that society has forgotten. Grant me the strength Father, to love other people as much as I love myself.

March 6

Know that you are God's temple and that God's spirit
dwells in you.

1 Corinthians 3:16

Reflection: Sin, by definition hurts other people but it also defiles us. Destroying our body with chemicals or with alcohol is not something that God approves of. As well, every time we act with unkindness or deceit, we dishonor Him, and we disrespect ourselves. The Bible tells us that whenever we do wrong, we vex the Holy Spirit. Jesus warned people against defiling the house of God, so we too must guard against bringing shame to the body that God gave us to wear. We are God's holy temple because God's spirit dwells in us.

Prayer: Father, thank You for blessing me with Your Spirit. May my body and soul always bring honor to You. Please forgive me for I have not always respected my body.

March 7

Out of place is obscene, silly, and vulgar talk; but instead let there be thanksgiving.

Ephesians 5:4

Reflection: Bad things start with small silly comments. How many times have we told unclean jokes or made what we consider to be harmless comments only to feel very uncomfortable afterwards? In fact, it is through such "harmless" comments that the devil finds a foothold. Jokes at the expense of other people, and tasteless comments which direct attention to defiling images, remain in our mind for a long time. We are reminded in the verse to watch what we say and to resist the temptation to speak out on everything that runs through our minds.

Prayer: Help me, Father, to remain sober at all times so that I never lose control of my words and say things which are hurtful to others.

March 8

Finally, brothers, whatever is true, whatever is noble, whatever is right, whatever is pure, whatever is lovely, whatever is admirable, if anything is excellent or praiseworthy, think about such things.

Philippians 4:8

Reflection: We see then that Jesus' teaching is not about doing terrible things to other people, or about spreading hate and rumors. Christian faith is about love and spiritual growth. Christians aim for noble things. We wish to follow Jesus not only because He alone bore our pain and wrongdoings, but also because His character is without blemish. A man of peace, of love, of compassion, of forgiveness; a gentleman is our teacher, Jesus. And there is no historical equal to Jesus in terms of human virtue. We should wake up every day and say "Today, I will bask in the glory of God."

Prayer: Lord, grant that I might reflect Your attributes in what I say and do, to the people I come across today, especially to those who have been marginalized.

March 9

*And the peace of Christ which guards all things will
guard your hearts and your minds in Christ Jesus.*

Philippians 4:7

Reflection: What is the use of knowing Jesus if we do not believe and
trust Him? If we were perfect we would have no need of anything.
But we come to Jesus because we want peace and we desire wisdom
and forgiveness. We come to know through experience, that the Holy
Spirit can find a home in our hearts. This is a great thing in that the
Spirit of God is not restricted by time or space as our physical body
is. The Spirit can accomplish great things on our behalf. The more we
live in the Spirit, the more we exist outside the physical laws of nature
and the more we can accomplish. Because Jesus was pure at heart,
He radiated power and glory and He told His disciples that they too
could do great works, if they were obedient. The peace of Christ is
worth our devotion.

Prayer: Jesus, help me and my family to enjoy Your peace today. I
pray that Christ's love will shine through me today to all those I come
across.

March 10

But those who hope in the Lord will renew their strength.
They will soar on wings like eagles, they will run and not
grow weary, they will walk and not be faint.

Isaiah 40:31

Reflection: A marathon race would be a piece of cake if we could rest and refresh as often as we wished along the way. In the marathon of life, we have a chance in Jesus to renew our strength as often as we need to. And so when others give up or lose hope, the Spirit of God keeps us going, refreshed all the way to the finish line! Why should we not take advantage of this opportunity? The devil loads his followers with pride and hate, while Jesus instills hope and trust in His followers so that they can be refreshed constantly. Jesus is our hope and strength.

Prayer: Lord, help me to take advantage of the refuge that only You can offer so that my body and soul are always fresh and able to continue the journey. Today I will not be weary, for I know that Jesus's love sustains me.

March 11

But in your hearts, set apart Christ as Lord. Always be prepared to give an answer to everyone who asks you to give the reason for the hope that you have. But do this with gentleness and respect.

1 Peter 3:15

Reflection: If your child asks you to list the qualities you like in Jesus, what would you say? Your response should be that the Teacher is about love and forgiveness. He is about helping us to use our tongues to build up others and not to destroy others. He is about sowing peace rather than hatred. He is about praying for those who persecute us. In short, we follow Jesus because we wish to become like Him. We have hope because our conscience testifies that what Jesus teaches is good, peaceful and life sustaining. And so our lives as Christians should be attractive to those around us and if we form the habit of bringing our questions to God then we will have answers for those who question our faith.

Prayer: Holy Spirit, please help me not only to reflect the love and wisdom of God, but also to know how to gently and lovingly explain Jesus to those who do not know Him. Today I will ask Jesus to help me understand some of the things that puzzle me about my life.

March 12

But seek first His kingdom and His righteousness, and
all these things will be given to you as well.

Matthew 6:33

Reflection: One of the reasons that we often lack faith is because we are looking for faith in the wrong place. Faith does not grow through philosophical debates. God is discovered through repentance and through a desire to be good and to gain understanding about spiritual matters. But we must be prepared to set aside our prejudices and assumptions. We must be prepared to be challenged by the teachings of Jesus. Life can be hard when we attempt to function without a good foundation. The best foundation available is one that was built by God Himself on His Son Jesus. The foundation that Jesus offers is built on love, faith, trust, and discipline. We must always put God first, by the way we interact with each other, the way we treat strangers, and the way we treat those who offend us.

Prayer: Spirit of God, please help me to never forget to put God's interests in all my decisions, in my thoughts, and in my aspirations. Today I will think about God before I make decisions.

March 13

We must keep our eyes on Jesus who leads us and makes our faith complete. He endured the shame of being nailed to a cross because He knew that later on, He would be glad He did. Now He is seated at the right side of God's throne.

Hebrews 12:2

Reflection: Students, athletes and trades people put up with hardship and deprive themselves of things because they know that one day they will become masters of their trade and will have better control over their economic future. Jesus suffered partly because he knew that one day we would finally return to God. And so we too if we desire God's grace and wisdom must be prepared to forgo some pleasures. But depriving ourselves of some earthly pleasures does not mean that life has to be boring. Real and lasting pleasure can be found in many good things in our world that are not contrary to God's teachings.

Prayer: Spirit of God, help me to understand what I must give up in order for me to carry my cross behind Jesus. Today I will choose to do Your will rather than seek bodily pleasures.

March 14

You are tempted in the same way that everyone else is tempted. But God can be trusted not to let you be tempted too much and He will show you how to escape from temptations.

1 Corinthians 10:13

Reflection: Sugar is a temptation that we too often give in to because it stimulates a pleasure area of the brain. But sugar causes a lot of problems, some of them serious problems. This is the nature of temptation in general. It provides short-term pleasure and leaves us with long term issues. God does not tempt anyone, we are tempted by our own desires. When our will is weak because we have strayed from prayer and devotion, the desire to stimulate short term pleasure areas of the brain becomes too strong for us to overcome. This verse highlights the fact that God makes it very difficult for us to sin by placing obstacles in the way. It is only after we persist that sin is allowed to overtake us.

Prayer: Spirit of God, help me stay focused in prayer so that I may be able to overcome temptations and so that my thoughts, my words and my actions may be pleasing to God. Today I pray that You will deliver me from temptation.

March 15

Blessed are the merciful, for they will receive mercy.

Matthew 5:7

Reflection: To show mercy is to turn away from the devil, who as we know delights in revenge. And yet sometimes an act is so wicked that it almost provokes instinctive revenge. But even then, we need to remember, that God is a witness to all wickedness that occurs. And God tells us that He will avenge on behalf of victims. Showing mercy, on the other hand, is a good way for us to rehabilitate those who offend us. Mercy diffuses situations, rather than escalating them. It is a lot easier to seek God's mercy when we too have shown mercy to others. There is a reason that Jesus said we are to forgive seventy seven times and that we are to pray for those who persecute us. Showing mercy and compassion has always been one of the things that sets Christians apart from many other faiths.

Prayer: Father God, I am sustained by Your mercy. May I always extend mercy to all I come across, so that people will know, that I am willing to follow in the steps of Jesus.

March 16

The harvest is great, the laborers few.

Luke 10:2-3

Reflection: The work of creation continues. There are many places in the world where people are not free to worship in accordance with their conscience. There are many places where people are shunned and spat on because they have chosen to follow the teachings of Jesus. There are people who still tell themselves that it is okay to hurt or kill people who do not share their faith. There are some cultures that burn Bibles and tell their children that Christians are their enemies. And so there is still a lot of work for those who love God. Hospitals, nursing homes, and prisons - these are some of the places where people need love and help. Jesus has opened our eyes and his teachings have civilized our hearts and so we are called by God to use what we know to awaken the conscience of others. Christians are called to help all people regardless of faith.

Prayer: Lord of the harvest, please grant me the privilege of working in Your vineyard and teach me to become a faithful disciple.

March 17 – Feast Day of St. Patrick of Ireland

———◦———

God planned for us to do good things and to live as He has always wanted us to live. That's why He sent Christ to make us what we are.

Ephesians 2:10

Reflection: How easily we forget that the life we now have is only a shadow of the life that God created us to have. Our spirits long ago existed without the physical limitations we now experience in the animal body we wear as humans. It was only after Adam and Eve disobeyed God that they realized their "nakedness". This nakedness was a physical reality which marked their disobedience. Today we exist both in spirit and in a physical form. Jesus came to lead us back to that pure state of total love and obedience to God. Christ's teachings will lead us to a state of total trust in God and to a life of helping others. Psychologists are now learning that people feel most fulfilled when they are helping other people. People who volunteer their time, or people who are the ones others turn to for help in difficult times, often speak of how good it feels to be there for others. Christ did so much good for us that His will is for us to do great things for each other.

Prayer: Spirit of God, help me to live a selfless charity-filled life, motivated by love as I journey back to a pure heart. Today I will not neglect the people around me who need my help.

March 18

Anyone who belongs to Christ is a new person. The past is forgotten, and everything is new.

2 Corinthians 5:17

Reflection: Belonging to Christ is like waking up from a dreary sleep. It means that we are prepared to renounce wickedness in all its forms. It also means that we are willing to subject ourselves to the teachings of Jesus as directed by the Holy Spirit. If we remain close to Jesus then we move forward. Even though we remain imperfect after we are born again, the Holy Spirit continues God's work in us. If we persist in wrongdoing, then we crucify Jesus all over again. A child of God does not keep on sinning. Thank God that the past is forgiven. We can demonstrate our gratitude by the way we live from this day on.

Prayer: Thank You, Jesus, for making me a new person and for counting me worthy to call God my Father. Today, I will live like a new person so that everyone I come across will see me as a new person reborn in Christ Jesus.

March 19

But understand this, that in the last days there will come times of difficulty. For people will be lovers of self, lovers of money, proud, arrogant, abusive, disobedient to their parents, ungrateful, unholy.

Timothy 3:1-2

Reflection: Young children are controlled by fear of their parents, but one day children will become adults and will be free to do as they please. Mature societies are less controlling and their citizens are free to live as they desire. This is part of the plan of creation and is not a bad thing because it is only when we are totally free to do as we please without any fear, that we learn who we are. Paul, in the above letter is talking about that time when civil laws are completely stripped of morality and each person is able to live as he pleases. The western world is almost there and the rest of the world not far behind. The pain and suffering which follows, will help humanity better appreciate the meaning of wickedness and the grace of God.

Prayer: Father, you have given me the ability to choose how I live. Help me to learn self-control so that I will only pursue those things which are good for me and for the world.

March 20

God's Spirit does not make cowards out of us. The Spirit gives us power, love, and self-control.

2 Timothy 1:7

Reflection: Too much self-love can create fear and too much desire to please other people can turn us into cowards. Apostle Peter denied knowing Jesus because he was afraid of what the authorities would do to him. When he completely put his trust in God, this fear went away. As much as we would like to, we can never be in total control of life and so whether we like it or not, we have to learn to trust in a greater power outside of ourselves (namely, God). When our cause is good, and our method is gentle, and when we pose no harm to others, then we should never be afraid to let people know that we love God or that we are grateful to Jesus for His love for us.

Prayer: Spirit of God, help me to be bold and wise, so that I may never be so fearful that I deny my love and adoration for Jesus. Help me to never choose a means to an end which does not meet with Your approval. Today I pray for the courage to live a life that is pleasing to God.

March 21

What God has said isn't only alive and active! It is sharper than any double-edged sword. This word can cut through our spirits and souls and through our joints and marrow, until it discovers desires and thoughts of our hearts.

Hebrews 4:12

Reflection: When we think back a few years and recall how we saw the world, then we begin to appreciate how little we really knew. Self-knowledge is one of the goals of life. God's Word, written in our hearts, enables us to discover who we are and to do something about the things we don't want. The teachings of Jesus are a mirror of what God already put in our hearts. Our experience on a daily basis also confirms to us that love is more fulfilling than hate, that mercy is more satisfying than revenge. From the beginning of humanity, the Holy Spirit kept alive the word of God through the Hebrew prophets, and today the Holy Spirit is alive in the Church, and in the people who submit their hearts to the teachings of Jesus. And so as we go about our daily activities we encounter spiritual lessons in the things and in the people we come across.

Prayer: Spirit of God, as you search my soul, give me the strength to learn from my past errors, so that I am never discouraged. Today I will bless those people I come across who spread the love of God.

March 22

But your sinful acts have alienated you from your God; your sins have caused Him to reject you and not listen to your prayers.

Isaiah 59:2

Reflection: There are people who "pray" fervently but still go around committing mass murder. Many terrorists pray daily. This verse tells us that sometimes living in sin can so alienate us from God that our prayer is just a one way affair. A hardened heart does not listen to God, it is bent on revenge. God has allowed us to know good and bad in order that we might freely choose good over evil. The only thing that can keep us from God is our own disobedience. And even though there is no reason why His energy should continue to sustain our bad choices, God's love for us is so profound that the Holy Spirit is here on a daily basis protecting and guiding us. God's will shall be done on Earth. God cannot fail and so, even if sometimes things appear bleak, He continues to move us towards perfect love and towards wisdom. What looks bleak today will emerge tomorrow as a period of advancement towards the Kingdom.

Prayer: Spirit of God, thank You for being here with me. May I never be separated from the love of God. Today I invite You to make me do the Will of God my Father.

March 23

God is the one who began this good work in you, and I am certain that he won't stop before it is complete on the day that Christ Jesus returns.

Philippians 1:6

Reflection: When we pray to God we have to take the time to listen. God has a purpose for each of us and unless we believe that God is not able to fulfill His promise, we have no reason to worry. Everyone learns and everyone grows in knowledge and wisdom, but we do so at different rates and in different areas. Even the worst drug addict is still learning a lesson or two about life. The easy way to learn is to discipline oneself and to pray regularly. This is how we make less costly mistakes daily. If we don't stop to pray and to reflect regularly then the mistakes we make becomes our primary teacher. This is a hard way to learn. It is a lot easier to grow by regularly talking to God and by following the examples of the saints. Even if we ignore God, life has been designed to teach us love and charity. Our salvation was completed on that day when Jesus was nailed to the cross.

Prayer: Spirit of God, help me to always give thanks and to appreciate the good work that You are carrying out in me. Today my heart will open so that I can learn things the easy way and not through pain.

March 24

But the hour is coming, and is now here, when the true
worshipers will worship the Father in spirit and truth,
for the Father is seeking such people to worship Him.

John 4:23

Reflection: To worship God means that we are devoted to His Word and respectful of His laws. We have all been in situations where we wished to convince someone about the existence of God, yet nothing we could come up with appeared to work. A surprising fact is that most people believe that we are not alone in the universe; many people believe in a "higher power", but are turned off by "organized "religion. People often have difficulty with the idea that God is found only in one religion and not in other religions. This is a legitimate concern. And one of the things about Christianity is that it is not a tribal religion. In fact, Jesus throughout his life on earth, drew everyone close to him, Jews, Romans, Samaritans, Greeks, Ethiopians, etc. The Christian religion is firstly about renouncing wickedness, then accepting the grace of God and becoming committed to learning how to love God and how to love other people. These basic teachings of our faith are not controversial or dishonorable.

Prayer: Spirit of God, guide me to a praying community that will help me to better realize my potential as a spiritual being. Today I will worship God in truth and in spirit.

March 25

*The thief comes only to steal and kill and destroy. I came
so that everyone would have life, and have it in its fullest.*

John 10:10

Reflection: The thief is Satan, the devil who preaches hate and violence, God's enemy, as well as ours. Followers of Jesus must be peace-loving like Jesus, and must share His love and compassion for people. Because of Jesus we do not have to return to a life of pain and isolation. Through Jesus, we will learn how to work hard, so we can be self-sufficient, and we will learn how to not take life for granted, so that we can more fully enjoy the beauty around us without crossing the line into sin. Only by listening to the Holy Spirit can we enjoy the quality of life that God has in store for us. This passage reminds us that Jesus has called everyone, and every nation. Satan comes to us in the guise of a friend, inviting us to have a little fun with him. But the thief delights in turning "a little fun" into addictive, destructive habits. The thief doesn't care, in fact this is what the thief hoped would happen. This verse invites us to be vigilant, to be careful of the smoke and mirror that the devil presents. We know that Jesus is the Good Shepherd because He preaches love, so we believe and trust in Him so that none of us fall prey to the devil's knavish tricks, and that none of us cause harm to ourselves or others.

Prayer: Lord, help me to find the life that you designed for me and help me to resist temptations all day long. Protect me from those who preach hate and any type of prejudice. Today I will be happy and full of cheer, I will laugh and rejoice all day long.

March 26

I praise you because I am fearfully and wonderfully
made; Your works are wonderful, I know that full well.

Psalm 139:14

Reflection: We have not begun to live until we learn to enjoy God's highest creation – other people. In fact the highest punishment known to us is banishment from society, removal from the midst of other people. Jesus was rarely alone. He enjoyed spending time with His disciples. The need to be around people never changes. What changes is our attitude. Envy, hypocrisy, and condemnation are some of the negative attitudes that keep us from enjoying other people. Whenever possible, take the time to chat with the bank teller, or with someone you meet in church. Speaking with other people can be very relaxing and is a great way to build a network for friendship or business. Everything that God has made is enjoyable, even the air we breathe.

Prayer: Lord, I thank You for my family and my friends. I thank You that today and every day, there are people that I can talk to, people I can visit, and people I can help. Today, I will take the time to appreciate the wonders of the world around me and to give thanks to the Creator.

March 27

Those who consider themselves religious and yet do not
keep a tight rein on their tongues deceive themselves, and
their religion is worthless

James 1:26

Reflection: This verse shows how crucial it is that we watch what comes out of our mouths. Is it gossip? Is it designed to cut someone down or to abuse someone? Our Lord disapproves of those who delight in spreading unpleasant information about other people. What we say can often hurt others more than physical violence. Furthermore, we should remember that when we are speaking, we are not thinking. If you observe your friends and families, you will see that those who guard their speech are more thoughtful and careful. It has been said that it is better to remain quiet and be thought of as a fool than to speak and remove all doubt.

Prayer: Father, teach me to use my mouth to build others up and to glorify Your Holy Name. May I never be known as the gossip, the one who says unkind things about people.

March 28

Some men came to Him, Jesus, bringing a paralyzed man.

Mark 2:3

Reflection: The presence of suffering is one reason that many people question the existence of God. Strangely though, it is rarely our personal pain or suffering which causes us to doubt God. When we read about the plight of sick children and their parents, we assume that their life is unfair, and that God does not exist. But if we ask the question: "Has life been fair or good to me?" the answer is usually yes! And so, rather than make assumptions about how others are doing or debating why you think God is unkind to others, we should bring our questions directly to God. "Why is there pain in my life?" "Why do people suffer?" These are good questions and there is no reason why we can't ask God. Anything that is a concern for us, God wants to hear it.

Prayer: Help me, Father, to see past the many assumptions I make regarding other people. I must learn to trust that You are with everyone, especially with those in pain. Today I will take my questions to You directly rather than jump to conclusions about the plight of others.

March 20

While they were stoning him, Stephen prayed, "Lord
Jesus, receive my spirit." Then he fell on his knees and
cried out, "Lord, do not hold this sin against them."

Acts 7: 59-60

Reflection: Stephen was so full of love and compassion that he begged
God for power to do wonders for his enemies. Where did Stephen's
love come from? Why was he able to keep praying even as people
stoned him to death? "Lord, forgive them, for they know not what they
do," he said as stones landed on him. Could we too do what Stephen
did? The answer is that yes we can, with the Holy Spirit, everything is
possible. Stephen became empowered by being receptive to the Holy
Spirit. When we are obedient to God, we are rewarded with a loving
heart.

Prayer: Spirit of God, use me to do wonders so that my friends and
family will witness Your love and mercy. Help me to bring a smile to
the face of everyone I meet today.

March 30

Love does no harm to its neighbor. Therefore, love is the fulfilment of the law.

Romans 13:10

Reflection: We are familiar with the Ten Commandments, but, in fact, there are hundreds of other commandments in the Bible. The laws in the Bible, as Jesus demonstrated, are to be exercised with love and forgiveness. God's laws were not given so we could use them to shame each other. We are all sinners. Thus, Jesus refused to stone an adulterer even though there was a command about it. Jesus preached forgiveness to others rather than to seek an eye for an eye. All of the commandments of God stem from love and love only. A parent is never happy to see one child harm his sister. And so God is dismayed when we harm our neighbor.

Prayer: Lord, teach me to focus all my actions on loving my neighbor as myself. Today I will bless my neighbor.

March 31

So could you not stay awake with me one hour?

Matthew 26:40

Reflection: We often forget that Jesus was fully human, in addition to being fully divine. As such, Jesus enjoyed the presence of others. Imagine the scene which gave rise to the above passage where Jesus was praying fervently while His apostles were snoring around him. As He said later, "the spirit is willing, but the flesh is weak." However, these same weak people, who could not stay awake to pray with their Master in His time of need, would later accept horrific deaths rather than renounce their faith in Jesus. What changed to make them so bold and strong? Jesus gave them the gift of the Holy Spirit. What is impossible for us is possible with God. We too have access to the power that turned weaklings into martyrs.

Prayer: Spirit of God, embolden and strengthen me so that I may always be awake and my Master may find me doing good work when he returns.

April 1

Blessed be the God and Father of our Lord Jesus Christ,
who according to His great mercy has caused us to be born
again to a living hope through the resurrection of Jesus
Christ from the dead.

1 Peter 1:3

Reflection: From a spiritual perspective, there are two stages of human development. During the first stage we do things more or less mindlessly, testing our limits and capabilities. The consequences are not that dire at this stage of life. It is as if God is stepping back and allowing us to see the extent of our own wickedness. For it is when we are entirely free to do as we please knowing there will be no consequences, that our basic nature is fully expressed. It is at the second stage of life that we are fully aware of an internal conscience which then begins to slowly hound us when we misbehave. This is when mental anguish follows bad behavior. At this junction of life we are called to make a decision on how we wish to spend the remainder of life. If we resolve to become spiritual and to submit to the laws of God, we then meet Jesus and begin to grow in wisdom and love; we are born again to a living hope.

Prayer: Lord, today, I repeat my desire to turn my will over to You so that the Holy Spirit might prepare and use me in Your service.

April 2

I am the true vine, and my father is the vine grower that removes every branch that bears no fruit.

John 15:1

Reflection: Jesus tells us in this passage that we are to carry our cross daily and work in the vineyard just like He did. We find Jesus, we repent, we are forgiven, then we learn and then we serve. The word of God became flesh and the flesh was Jesus and now through Jesus the Word is passed on to us so we can work in God's Kingdom. Let us bear fruits by modelling goodness and devotion to others so that we are not cut off from Jesus and our energy passed on to those who would make better use of it. Energy is from God and is never destroyed; it can only be transformed. What we should desire is for God to pour His energy onto us so that we can be effective in serving one another. We don't want to be guilty of wasting God's energy.

Prayer: Lord, help me to discipline my days and nights so that I may carry my cross daily and bear fruits in your kingdom. May the energy that You have given me bear great fruit.

April 3

*Sir, give me a drink of that water! Then I won't get thirsty
and have to come to this well again.*

John 4:15

Reflection: Jesus asked a Samaritan woman He met at the well
for water. The woman responded by telling Jesus that Jews did not
interact with non-Jews. During the time of Jesus, and even today,
people thought they knew who belonged to God. Jesus showed by His
interaction with the Samaritan woman that God remains accessible to
all people even to those who have sinned over and over. The woman at
the well had been married many times and was a Samaritan. Ancient
Jews regarded her as outside of God's call. Yet, she had the privilege
of meeting face to face with the Son of God. Jesus has indeed brought
salvation to all nations. Hallelujah!

Prayer: Thank You, God, for adopting me as Your child. I was once
lost and hopeless but Jesus has made a home for me in Your mansion.
Today I will celebrate knowing that You are my father.

April 4

This woman belongs to the family of Abraham and Satan has kept her bound for eighteen years. Isn't it right to set her free on the Sabbath?

Luke 13:16

Reflection: The idea behind the Sabbath is that it is to be a day of rest when no work should be done. God wanted to remind people that it is good to rest from work. But Jesus reminded his critics that it is more important to set this woman free immediately rather than wait for the Sabbath to be over. Sometimes we lose focus on what is really important and become too rigid. Jesus, by healing a sick woman on the Sabbath, reminds us that when our goals conflict, we have to choose the more important goal, always bearing in mind, however, that in this specific sort of situation, the end does justify the means. It is dangerous to be legalistic when applying laws.

Prayer: Spirit of God, soften my heart so that I may not be a hypocrite and become rigid in applying laws and rules my way.

April 5

Keep your eyes focused on what is right and look straight ahead to what is good.

Proverbs 4:25

Reflection: There is no easier way to invite trouble than for a married or attached person to cultivate a wandering eye. Falling in love with someone other than one's own spouse doesn't occur by accident; it starts with a wandering eye. The more we keep our eyes straight, the longer we keep appreciating the person we are committed to. But the point of the passage is that we should not envy people around us who may be struggling with things we have left behind. Instead we are to focus our thoughts on what is good so that we can keep growing.

Prayer: Spirit of God, help me to keep my eyes focused on my responsibilities as a spouse and as a parent. May I never bring disharmony to my family. Today I will endeavor to keep my eyes straight.

April 6

They are gossips, slanderers...

Romans 1:29

Reflection: If no one listened to gossip, or read gossip in the newspapers, then there would be no gossip. We feel hurt when others gossip about us, even if what they say is true. Gossip causes strife and discord; it breaks up friendships. We often justify gossip by telling ourselves that we are only just repeating something everyone already knows or that we are only making an observation. If we don't appreciate others spreading stories about us, then we should not discuss others behind their back. The verse invites us to change the topic or to walk away next time someone starts to gossip.

Prayer: Spirit of God, please help me to control my tongue so that I may use it to build others up rather than to tear them down. Today I will not listen to any gossip either verbally or in print.

April 7

*Do not stop him; for no one who does a deed of power
in My name will be able soon afterward to speak evil of
Me. Whoever is not against us is for us.*

Mark 9:39

Reflection: The disciples of Jesus believed at one point that only
people who went around with them should have the power to heal
the sick, and so when they saw a man healing people in the name of
Jesus, they were ready to stop him. Jesus himself ran into difficulties
with religious leaders who questioned His pedigree. These religious
leaders believed that Jesus, whose observable father was Joseph the
carpenter, had no business calling himself the Son of God. Jesus was
not even born into a priestly family. It is common for all of us to think
we know who is in or out with God. But Jesus showed us over and
over that we really don't know. Our duty is to love and to reflect the
mercy of God, not to decide who has favor with God or who has the
right to proclaim Him.

Prayer: Father, only You know who has found favor with You. May
I never stand in the way of those You have sent to spread Your word.

April 8

*The Lord watches over the way of the righteous, but the
way of the wicked will perish.*

Psalm 1:6

Reflection: The righteous are those people who are repentant and
are willing to be guided by the Holy Spirit. It is not easy for anyone to
perish! The Holy Spirit goes the extra mile to help, to teach, to prod,
or to cajole, to do whatever it takes for us to come to our senses, short
of taking away our free will. But at the end of the day, we retain the
choice to heed the teaching of God or to live like animals. What God
wants for us is what we should want for ourselves – a life of discipline
in which we pose no issues for others and a life in which we are willing
to repent and to grow. As far as we know animals perish and their
elements are recycled. The Bible warns us that unless we repent we
stand in danger of perishing.

Prayer: Holy Spirit, please watch over my ways, help me to remain
calm today so that I will not entertain bad thoughts, do the wrong
things or say the wrong things.

April 9

Too much pride will destroy you.

Proverbs 16:18

Reflection: Hard work and discipline can bring success and pride. Pride is one of the things that the devil would like to give each of us. Pride is what causes us to be rude to others and keeps us from apologizing when we are wrong. Pride is what makes us forget that a privileged life must be lived with great humility and service. Pride is what causes us to stop listening to others and to forget how to learn and how to make lasting friendships. Pride makes us believe that we deserve more respect than others and, as the Bible tells us, pride destroys people. Those in high places will honor God by being humble and accessible to other people. This is the example of Jesus.

Prayer: Spirit of God, teach me humility and help me to never forget that we all deserve equal respect. Help me to use my position to serve rather than to bully. Today, I will show humility in all my dealings with people.

April 10

Whenever people are jealous or selfish, they cause trouble and do all sorts of cruel things.

James 3:16

Reflection: From time to time we experience jealousy. But when we become so jealous that we are negative, then we are in danger of causing trouble. Envy is what makes us believe that when good fortune comes to a neighbor, then we have been hard done by! It is true that most of us would rather see a stranger win the lottery than a friend, unless of course the friend is willing to share his winnings with us. Rather than envy people it is better to form the habit of imitating what we admire in them. Successful people prefer to learn from other people rather than wish them bad. Next time you feel envious or jealous, pray for the wisdom and strength to not feel that way.

Prayer: Spirit of God, help me to be happy when my neighbor meets with good fortune. Teach me to focus on my strengths rather than the perceived strength of my neighbor. Today I will pray for those who make me feel insecure.

April 11

———◦◦◦———

*The soul of the sluggard craves and gets nothing while the
soul of the diligent is richly supplied.*

Proverbs 13:4

Reflection: It is painful to have so little and to want so much,
especially if our poverty comes from laziness or slackness. There
is joy in a job well done. When we study hard or take our tasks
seriously enough, we begin to enjoy the time we spend on the task.
Professionals, trades people, firefighters, hockey players, even tax
collectors – these are examples of people who have applied themselves
to learn their profession well and who work hard to benefit us all. If
we apply ourselves, we too can reach the top of our chosen field. The
devil delights in lazy people, while God may be disappointed when
we neglect to utilize our gifts to benefit society.

Prayer: Spirit of God, help me to find joy in my work and help me to
make the best of the gifts God has given me. Today, I will work hard
at every task I am assigned.

April 12

I will never leave you, I will never abandon you.

Hebrews 13:5

Reflection: God chose to create us so that we can experience the joy of life and to learn love. God is with us every step of the way and who knows us better than God? "Going it alone" without God, isn't easy. It is filled with wasted days and lost opportunities. Going it alone often means that we place ourselves as having become our own God. We are all guilty of this at one time or another. The result of ignoring our spirituality is that life becomes weary, hurried, and tiring. We are always anxious; never having time for anything or anyone. Yet if we take just a little time daily to quietly connect with the Holy Spirit in prayer – we seem to gain more time. Priorities change, anxiety is reduced, and we are more at peace. God will never abandon us even if we reject His help.

Prayer: Lord, when I consider the mess that we have made of Your beautiful world, I realize that we cannot function at our best without your guidance. Help me Lord, to not become arrogant, and think I know better than You.

April 13

For My thoughts are not your thoughts, neither are your ways my ways, declares the Lord. For as the heavens are higher than the earth, so are My ways higher than your ways and My thoughts than your thoughts.

Isaiah 55:8-9

Reflection: Young children love sweets and they can never understand why their parents do not allow them to indulge. One of the difficulties we all encounter is trying to make sense of life. We see good people suffer and die and we see people who are not so good prosper in good health. Life sometimes makes no sense and we often feel that we have nowhere to turn to for answers. We have all wondered why it is that God allows suffering; why children die of starvation; why innocent people are killed by bombs. One thing that we can be certain of is that there is more to life than meets the eye. The human mind can only glimpse a small aspect of life at a time. When Jesus was here he answered the questions that were posed to him. And so it is a mistake to think that we cannot take our questions to God. There is no question too small, no question, too silly and no question too big for God. All we have to do is ask and then be prepared to listen and to learn.

Prayer: Lord, help me to always examine my assumptions and beliefs so that I might always be open to a new understanding of what my life is about. Today I will take my questions to God so that I might learn more things.

April 14

Do you not believe I am in the Father and the Father is in Me?

John 14:10

Reflection: The Trinity of God is a mystery that has baffled people over the ages. Are there three gods or one God? It is easier to begin to understand the Trinity when we realize that we too are three beings in one. First we resemble great apes in physicality; but we also have an inner voice which tells us good from bad; and our third component is the consciousness which carries out our actions. Jesus is in the Father and the Father is in Him, just as we are in the physical form and the physical form is in us. Jesus was not just a prophet or a good preacher. He was the visible form of God. There is only one God consisting of the Son that was visible, the Holy Spirit, not visible but perceived in other ways, and the Father, analogous perhaps to human consciousness.

Prayer: Father, help me to focus on the teachings which help me to grow in wisdom and love so that my mind may not be diverted to things beyond my understanding.

April 15

---◁◦▷---

Very truly, I tell you, anyone who hears my word and believed Him who sent me has eternal life, and does not come under judgment, but has passed from death to life.

John 5:24

Reflection: Why do some people believe the teachings of Jesus when others reject it? The simple answer is choice. Many people who value love and forgiveness readily embrace the teachings of Jesus. We can choose to lead a life of love and forgiveness, a life in which we seek the help of the Holy Spirit in making amends for past mistakes. Or we can approach spirituality as simply a human construct with no consequences. Or we can look at religion as a competition between cultures and stubbornly hold on to the tradition of our ancestors even after we learn that the teaching of Jesus makes sense. The words of Jesus lead us away from wickedness and from death. It is easy for people who are willing to submit to the Spirit, to profess the goodness of the Lord. But we know that Christ died for all, so in due course, we believe that the teachings of Jesus will be universally embraced.

Prayer: Father God, I invite you to come into my heart and to make me do your will. Show me your way and I will follow the path that you show me even if it means following in the footsteps of Jesus.

April 16

When you are disturbed, do not sin; ponder it on your beds and be silent.

Psalm 4:4

Reflection: When we act out in anger we are almost certain to regret our actions. Anger comes out of false pride and insecurity. The anger and annoyance we feel often turn out to be evidence of a still maturing spirit, rather than evidence of wickedness in others. Scripture, as this verse demonstrates, is about helping us to live life more fully. This verse reminds us that we are better to remain silent and allow time to pass, before we respond, when we feel disturbed.

Prayer: Lord, please teach me to dwell on Your teachings day and night so that my mistakes are few and far between.

April 17

*If anyone of you have never sinned, then go ahead and
throw the first stone...*

John 8:7

Reflection: It is so easy to point the finger at someone else when we
may be just as guilty. The closer we get to God, the more we realize
that we are no better than other people. We are all saved by grace. And
so, God is not pleased when we judge other people. God does not want
us to be hypocrites. If we are truly interested in assisting the Holy
Spirit, then we are to use love to change people. Judgment belongs to
God because He understands each person's circumstances. We live in
glass houses and so we throw stones at our peril.

Prayer: Lord, help me to remove the log in my own eyes so that I can
better see my shortcomings. Today I will focus on my relationship
with Jesus.

April 18

Be glad even if you have a lot of trouble. You know that
you learn to endure by having your faith tested. But
you must learn to endure everything so that you will
completely mature and not lack in anything.

James 1:2-8

Reflection: It is difficult to be glad when we are in trouble. The point
of this verse is that we need to realize that trouble may mean that some
choice we made in the past, has come home to roost. In this sense,
trouble provides us with an opportunity to learn and to grow. Even
when we bring trouble upon ourselves, lessons from these troubles
often benefit those around us. Parents who are experiencing lung
problems as a result of nicotine damage show their children why they
should not take up smoking. There are hardly any issues in our lives
that do not hold lessons for us and for our children. As well, much of
what we experience in life helps us to build empathy for others and to
understand what others are experiencing. Trouble also brings us closer
to the things that are important to us and to God. The point is that God
uses our troubles especially when self-inflicted, to bring about good for
us and for others.

Prayer: Spirit of God, help me to bear the troubles that come my
way, and whatever lessons come with my troubles. Help me to also
understand these lessons.

April 19

Then Jesus used His story to teach His followers that they should always pray and never lose hope.

Luke 18.1

Reflection: Why pray? After all, God knows what we need or what we desire even before we pray. Prayer helps to call to mind the things that are important to us and what it is that keeps us from our goals. Prayer, especially when it comes from the heart, also helps us to connect with the Spirit of God. Prayer, as Jesus implies, gives us hope so that we might remain positive. But above all, prayer is our plea to the Father for special dispensation. Anyone accustomed to praying knows this. Prayer reinforces our faith and helps us to dispel the fear and anxiety that the evil one wishes to sow in us.

Prayer: Spirit of God, teach me how to pray so that I might never lose hope and so that I might reflect hope to people that I come across. Today I will not allow my mind to fear or to fall into despair.

April 20

Slow to anger, abounding in love and faithfulness, maintaining love to thousands and forgiving wickedness, rebellion, and sin. Yet He does not leave the guilty unpunished; He punishes the children and their children for the sins of the father to the third or fourth generation.

Exodus 34:6-7

Reflection: It is true that we carry the good and bad genes of our parents and it is true that if we grow up in a home with drugs, alcohol, and other issues, we are also affected. And so in this sense we are touched by the disobedience of people around us. But God does not bind us to this background in any way. We are always free to choose our own path and God provides the means and opportunities for us to be free to make our own choices. It is our choices which determine the life we live. In the end, we answer only for our choices.

Prayer: Lord, help me to forgive my parents and to love them unconditionally. I pray that they will become devoted to You just like I am trying to be. Today I will rejoice in Your kindness.

April 21

*The Pharisees and the Sadducees came and to test Jesus,
they asked him to show them a sign from heaven.*

Matthew 16:1

Reflection: 'Move this cup and I will believe in you!' This is a game
most of us have played. But mature people know that faith comes from
doing the things of the heart and being committed to growth. What is
required from us is a willingness to yield to the Spirit as we learn about
ourselves. When we begin to do thus, faith follows. If it were a matter
of a sign from heaven, we might as well demand that God appear to us
in physical form. When we do as we should, the Spirit removes the fog
which clouds our understanding of God. There are signs all around us
and we just need to open our hearts to perceive them.

Prayer: Father, I understand that what I perceive about life has more
to do with where I am on my spiritual journey than what is actually
out there. Help me to remain humble and open so that I may better
understand the mysteries around me.

April 22

And pray in the Spirit in all occasions with all kinds of
prayers and requests.

Ephesians 6:18

Reflection: Imagine how much life will change for the better if only
we could pray for just thirty minutes daily? This is less than the time
we spend eating daily. We all have a lot we wish to change in life.
Children, grandchildren, parents, siblings – this is just a small list of
people we wish well and people we can pray for daily. The more we
pray the better off we are and the closer we get to God. God is the
ultimate provider and so we should never hesitate to take all requests
to God, even if we think these requests are trivial.

Prayer: Spirit of God, help me to find the strength and discipline to
become devoted to daily prayer. Today I will make a list of my requests
to my Father.

April 23

Oh, taste and see that the Lord is good; blessed is the man who trusts in Him.

Psalm 34:8

Reflection: It often takes discord to make us appreciate how good we have it. Life, family, health, friends, nature – these are all gifts that we regularly take for granted. We all covet a life of total independence but the irony is that if we draw closer to God by living a more disciplined life, our quality of life improves so much. It is only by drawing closer that we come to appreciate life more fully. If we can't trust in God, who can we trust in?

Prayer: Lord, help me to taste life more fully. I pray that it would not take misfortune to make me appreciate all that you have given me. Today I will trust in God with all of my heart and all my soul.

April 24

And he said, "There was a man who had two sons. And the younger of them said to his father, 'Father, give me the share of property that is coming to me.' And he divided his property between them. Not many days later, the younger son gathered all he had and took a journey into a far country, and there he squandered his property in reckless living. And when he had spent everything, a severe famine arose in that country, and he began to be in need.

Luke 15:11-14

Reflection: When a prodigal son returns to his parents he must be washed clean and retaught the attributes of his parents. Sometimes, when we become devoted to a prayer life, we become more aware of our shortcomings. We too are being washed by the Holy Spirit. This is good in that, with more knowledge, come greater opportunities for change. Life has been calculated so that everything that happens to us, which at first blush, may seem to be mere coincidence, actually brings us closer to the reality of God. We are all called to a purpose by God.

Prayer: Spirit of God, open my eyes that I may see clearer and help me to trust that the disappointments of today are tomorrow's blessings. Today I will answer Your call, my Lord and my God.

April 25

I am weary with my moaning; every night I flood my bed
with tears; I drench my couch with my weeping.

Psalm 6:6

Reflection: Jesus once told the story of a woman who pestered a judge who was known to be often unfair, until that judge was so tired of her that he granted her wish to obtain just redress in her claim. God is good and God is not unfair. There are people in monasteries who pray for God's forgiveness day and night. Jesus was human, also, and he prayed constantly. Tears flow in us sometimes because we realize the extent of God's love for us. And sometimes they flow when we encounter people who have given up so much to follow Jesus. We too are invited to talk with God day and night. We are free to beg until our tears of sorrow become tears of joy.

Prayer: Father, sometimes I am lost for words, but I know that the spirit within me pleads my case without end. May I learn to love You deeper.

April 26

Answer me when I call, O Lord of my right! You gave me room when I was in distress. Be gracious to me and hear my prayer.

Psalm 4:1

Reflection: Few things are more distressing than human misery. And no one cares about us more than God. He listens to the prayers of every one of His children because He cares for us and He loves us so much. Even in trying times, God is there, holding our hands and listening to the words of our hearts. We may feel alone and abandoned whenever we experience hardships and trials, but each problem and every struggle are but opportunities that God uses to teach us valuable lessons in life. By going through seemingly hopeless situations, we emerge wiser, we become more resilient, we develop deeper empathy and love for others, and our faith in God grows stronger. Every prayer is answered with a bonus – patience.

Prayer: Spirit of God, I know that You always hear me. Thank You for teaching me patience as You help me to work through my prayers.

April 27

If you continue in My word, you are truly My disciples and you will know the truth and the truth will make you free.

John 8:31

Reflection: Human life can be compared to a book of mathematics broken down into chapters. Only after we understand the first chapter can we move on to the next one, and so on. Similarly human life unfolds chapter by chapter. It is only after we deal with one issue that the next one becomes obvious. Jesus teaches that if we do not continue in His teachings, and we quit along the way, there is a danger that we will fail to understand the truth. To grasp the truth is to reach a point where our singular desire is to love God and to love each other. Love drives away fear and where there is no fear there is freedom.

Prayer: Holy Spirit, please help me to abide in Jesus by regularly following my devotion plans. And help me to abide in Jesus until I see Him face to face.

April 28

Bless those who persecute you; bless and do not curse them.

Romans 12:14

Reflection: If we believe in God then we must believe that God is able to change the heart of those who persecute us. Jesus, even when he was about to die, prayed for his oppressors. Stephen prayed for those who were stoning him to death. Saul of Tarsus was present when Stephen was being stoned and he provided assistance to his killers. Saul was one of those that Stephen prayed for. Saul was saved by grace and he became Paul. A man who helped kill a follower of Jesus became a man who gave up his life to preach the teachings of Jesus to the world. The verse above came from Paul's letter to believers in Rome, who were being killed. History tells us that the blood of these martyrs became seed for the growth of Christianity. It was the same Romans who killed Christians for sport who were instrumental in spreading the faith across the world

Prayer: Father, thank You for my children, thank You for my spouse, and thank You for my co-workers. They teach me how to love and forgive.

April 29

Guard me as the apple of the eye; hide me in the shadow of your wings.

Psalm 17:8

Reflection: Jesus treated everyone, rich or poor, man or woman, tax collector or thief, with equal dignity and care. But we can be excused for wishing to be the one who is special to God, the favorite in God's family. Even after we reach adulthood, we remain as children before God. And so we are still prone to temptations and to disobedience. But where we are weak God is strong. As Christians, we believe that a living God oversees life on Earth and that God is able to keep us from trouble. We believe in a God who is not bound by time or space, a God who can do anything. This is an extraordinary faith. And so anyone receiving shelter from Him is blessed beyond measure. The good news is that we all are under the shadow of God's wings.

Prayer: When I sleep, allow me sweet dreams Lord, and when I wake, keep me faithful on the road set out by my Savior, Jesus.

April 30

The Lord is a stronghold for the oppressed, a stronghold in times of trouble.

Psalm 9:9

Reflection: Those who depend on God to fight their battles are in the best position. They do not resort to violence which too often hurts innocent people, instead they win their enemies over. Vengeance is mine, says the Lord. So long as we don't repay evil with evil or an eye for an eye, the Holy Spirit is our comforter and friend. When we are oppressed unjustly, we can count on the peace of God and His help in softening the heart of the oppressor. God also uses such difficulties to help us understand the plight of others. The important thing is that we should not wait for trouble to start before we seek refuge in God.

Prayer: Spirit of God, You are my refuge and strength. In times of trouble and in times of peace, Lord, may I abide in You when I am happy, and even when I am not so happy.

May 1

*Anyone, then, who knows the right thing to do and fails
to do it, commits sin.*

James 4:17

Reflection: One of the weaknesses of the atheist position is the failure
to explain the origin of evil and what we can do to eliminate it from
the world. There is no doubt that people sometimes do evil and are
hounded by conscience. If life is entirely about survival of the fittest,
then why do we feel guilt? No parent is happy knowing that a child
has done something that she knew was unacceptable. We as adults
know good from bad and we have the free will to choose which one we
do. But why then do we sometimes choose bad? Maybe we are selfish
or maybe we are vengeful. The point is that we have no valid excuse
for sin because God's laws written in our hearts are fair and obvious.
Because we all sin, we have Jesus to thank for pleading our case before
God and for ensuring that we receive pardons upon repentance. Doing
the right thing enables us to live a more fulfilled life in the spirit. And
so we see that Christianity explains that sin is the result of human
choices, and Christianity offers a solution for our redemption.

Prayer: Father God, help me to always strive to do the right thing so
that I may never be the source of pain and misery to others. Today I
will pay attention to my conscience.

May 2

And a harvest of righteousness is sown in peace for
those who make peace.

James 3:18

Reflection: Peace is harmony between people. To achieve peace,
sometimes everybody wins, but sometimes one side gets the better
of the other side. God values peace amongst people and where there
is love there is peace. The devil delights in us not getting along with
each other. And we play into the devil's hands when we forget that
other people are capable of feeling the same pain we would feel when
there is violence. At the root of most violence is the desire by one
party to exploit or dominate another group. Those who are exploited
can always count on Jesus to be on their side. Turning the other cheek
produces less violence. A harvest of righteousness, as the verse states,
comes through peace and so we must strive to look past short-term
gains and exploitation of other people, and seek lasting peace. Lasting
peace can only come when we respect and love each other and when
we are willing to give up our selfish desires for God's Holy ways.

Prayer: Lord, help me understand my prejudices so that I may not
interject myself unjustly into other people's disputes. Use me to sow
peace where there is hatred. Today I will pray for peace in our world.

May 3

What good is it, my brothers and sisters, if you say you have faith but do not have works?

James 2:14

Reflection: To have faith is to appreciate the goodness of the Lord. To appreciate God is to understand the significance of love and charity. When we commit to a life in the Spirit, we are cleansed and built up. We learn new things about who we are and we gain a new appreciation for life. In short, we become well equipped to relate to others, especially those going through things that we have already experienced. And so faith without charity will weaken. We are blessed with faith not just for our benefit but also for the benefit of others. Our faith should propel us to serve the interests of others.

Prayer: Lord, help me to show my faith by how I respond to those who require my help. May my actions help to build my faith as well as theirs.

May 4

Each is given the manifestation of Spirit for the common good.

1 Corinthians 12:7

Reflection: All good things come from God. There are many attributes that God wishes to share with us. We are different from every other person on earth and our experience is like no other in the world. So the gifts that we receive from the Holy Spirit are unique and are meant to fill particular needs in the vineyard of the Lord. Several trades are involved in building a house. No matter how skilled the carpenter is, the house is incomplete without the electrician. And so the kingdom of God is incomplete until we each contribute our gifts.

Prayer: Help me, Spirit of God, to develop my gifts, and to offer them selflessly to others for the common good.

May 5

*For you are not a God who delights in wickedness; evil
will not sojourn with you.*

Psalm 5:4

Reflection: No one has ever shown that the teachings of Jesus cause unfairness in the world. On the contrary humankind has been softened by the life of Jesus. Christianity is not a tribal religion which divides people superficially. If it were, it would not have such a wide appeal. Our faith tells us that all people are children of God and deserve to be treated fairly and with respect even when they do not share our faith. Our faith does not create a class of people as many false teachings do. We are called to be holy, because our Father is holy. Jesus was a man of peace, urging people to pray for oppressors. Mercy and forgiveness highlighted Jesus' interactions with people. No one who has ever tasted the goodness of the Lord can attribute anything but love to our Creator.

Prayer: Jesus, I am proud to call You Master because Your life is the best example of love and compassion that I know of. May I always be faithful to Your teachings so that goodness and mercy shall follow me all the days of my life.

May 6

Humble yourself before the Lord and He will exalt you.

James 4:10

Reflection: Next time you find yourself doing a good deed, take a minute or two to examine your motives, try to determine the one single thing that made you do it. When we are humble we do not become complacent, and this means that we do not disrespect other people. Humble people listen to other peoples' point of view without passing judgment. It is difficult to make too many enemies when we are humble. Patience is a sign of humility. Pride on the other hand causes us to say disrespectful things about other people and to seek to be the center of attention. All those who humbled themselves before Jesus were treated with honor. The more we know ourselves, the more we realize that any good we do originates from God. This is a humbling fact and so we can never boast about how good we are.

Prayer: Father God, I have been told that insecurity makes one become prideful. Help me to respect my brothers and sisters so that I do not seek to be held in higher regard. Father, I pray that I do not take credit for all the good things You have done for me.

May 7

There is only one lawgiver and judge who is able to save and to destroy. So who, then, are you to judge your neighbor?

James 4:12

Reflection: Our judgment on each other often arises from envy; it is often the case that we say one thing to a person and then criticize them behind their back. And we enjoy passing judgment on other people. Passing judgment on others, may make us feel good but it doesn't take away our faults. There is nothing wrong with pointing out mistakes to each other, so long as it is done out of love and not out of a sense of superiority. It is a sin to say bad things, or to think unfriendly things, about people.

Prayer: Father God, I know that only You are in a position to pass judgment on people, help me to resist the temptation to think of myself as better than others. Today, with the help of the Holy Spirit, I will refrain from thinking negative things about people.

May 8

Do not let the sun go down on your anger, and do not make room for the devil.

Ephesians 4:26

Reflection: Anger is like a seed that germinates and bears fruit, given enough time. It is amazing how long we hang on to anger. Simmering with pride and nursing anger only creates an opportunity for the devil to stoke the fire of hatred. Anger robs us of peace and makes us seek revenge. And the longer we continue to seethe in anger, the more our judgment becomes clouded, and the more we open ourselves up to the encouragement of the devil who enjoys conflicts among friends. Acting in anger makes us say and do things that we come to regret. Anger, like most negative forces, originates from pride, and pride, as we know, does not come from God.

Prayer: Father, I understand that anger comes from pride. Help me to remain humble so that I do not regard disagreements as personal affronts. For Your sake, Father, today I promise to let go of any anger that I might experience.

May 9

Resist the devil and he will flee from you.

James 4:7

Reflection: The devil is like a poisoned needle. If we keep our distance we can't be pricked, but if we come too close we stand the danger of being injected by his poison. On our own we are no match for the devil's trickery and so it is important that we do not give him room or time. We resist the devil by not inquiring into things that are sketchy and by not being nosey about dubious things that other people may be engaged in. We resist the devil by guiding our thoughts and not letting them wander onto bad subjects. "Curiosity killed the cat," the saying goes. Next time something negative occurs to you, dismiss it promptly and watch the devil flee from you. As well, "always speak the truth and let the devil be ashamed"!

Prayer: Spirit of God, take away my curiosity on things that are evil or wicked. Today I promise to keep my eyes straight and not to let them wander.

May 10

*If our hearts do not condemn us, we have boldness
before God.*

1 John 3:21

Reflection: God sees everything we do and so do we. Because we have a moral compass built in us everything we do is subject to evaluation by our conscience. Conscience is concerned with our motives and so even when we do something that turns out wrong, our conscience may not condemn us. But our conscience is very restless whenever we are about to do wrong, it tells us to think twice. If we end up doing wrong, then our conscience will condemn us afterwards. Guilt can create a neurotic sort of restlessness in us, and when guilt becomes too large, it can completely drown out our inner voice, thereby reducing us to an animal state of instincts. Jesus in this passage highlights the role that our conscience plays in keeping us from God. When Adam sinned he lost his boldness and hid from God.

Prayer: Spirit of God, create in me a lasting desire to listen to my inner voice so that I do not run afoul of the laws of God and hide from God.

May 11

*Blessed is anyone who endures temptation. Such a one
who has stood the test will receive the crown of life that
the Lord has promised to those who love him.*

James 1:12

Reflection: On our own, we will be kicked around by sin and
temptations. It is the Holy Spirit that ultimately enables us to resist
temptation. The Holy Spirit does this by teaching us about our
weaknesses and how best to overcome them and how best to respond
to bad habits. This might mean, for example, that we resolve to say a
prayer every time we are angry, so that we do not say or do things we
will regret. Temptation never goes away. Daily we make choices which
involve good and bad things. Every choice we make comes with a
lesson. If we make the wrong choice, we learn why it is wrong and we
remain at that level, until we commit to do better. On the other hand,
if we make a good choice, we also see why it was the best choice and
we move on to the next thing to be overcome. With the assistance of
the Holy Spirit, our journey back to God, is doable, and can actually
be fun.

Prayer: Father, help me move along efficiently along the path paved
by Your Son so that I will not be distracted by sin and spend too much
time learning the same things over and over.

May 12

Yes, everything else is worthless when compared with the infinite value of knowing Christ Jesus my Lord. For his sake I have discarded everything else, counting it all as garbage, so that I could gain Christ and become one with him...I want to know Christ and experience the mighty power that raised him from the dead.

Philippians 3:7-9

Reflection: The above letter by Paul gives us a glimpse of his religious conviction. Paul was a zealot with an unwavering desire to serve God. His background was Jewish, and he persecuted Jesus' followers when he thought he was doing the will of God. When he became an Apostle of Jesus he did not consider himself to be a convert from Judaism to Christianity. Paul merely came to see that Jesus was the Messiah that Hebrew prophets spoke of. Paul never met Jesus before the crucifixion, his change came after the Lord appeared to him If we too desire like Paul to follow God and to serve Him, the Holy Spirit will reveal the truth to us.

Prayer: Lord, thank You for Apostle Paul. His life showed that whoever desires to do the will of God, will rejoice in Your teachings. Today, Lord, I pray that I too will experience the mighty power that raised Jesus from the dead.

May 13

O Lord, do not rebuke me in your anger or discipline me in your wrath.

Psalm 6:1

Reflection: There is no greater love than the love that God has for us. But anyone that knows the Might of God must shudder at the thought of displeasing God. When our conscience condemns us, we are right to fear the Lord. God, however, is always interested in teaching and in growing our hearts, rather than in condemnation or punishment. A contrite heart, the Lord never rejects. And so, just as we sin daily, we are wise to pray daily and to take every opportunity to sing God's praise. No one is more worthy of adoration than our Father God.

Prayer: Lord, thank You for being gentle with me and thank You for not letting me feel the pain that I deserve. May my heart adore You forever.

May 14

Blessed are those whose iniquities are forgiven and those whose sins are covered.

Romans 4:8

Reflection: A woman told her priest that she saw Jesus in her dream. The skeptical clergyman said to her: "When next Jesus appears to you, ask Him to tell you what my sins are." The next Sunday, the woman told the clergyman she had again seen Jesus. "Did He tell you my sins?" he asked. "Yes," the woman responded, "Jesus told me to tell you that He forgot your sins the day He forgave you." The Bible tells us that all have sinned and fallen short of the glory of God and so we all need forgiveness. This verse illustrates how we too are to forgive others. To forgive is to forget.

Prayer: Spirit of God, teach me to forgive and forget just like Jesus forgave me.

May 15

The prayer of the righteous is powerful and effective.

James 5:16

Reflection: Any parent knows how difficult it is to say "no" to a favourite child. The prayer of Jesus on our behalf rises swiftly before God. As for us, when we become obedient to the will of God, we have the promise of Jesus, that whatever we ask in Jesus' name shall be granted. This is at the root of intercession prayers. In times of need we ask others to pray for us, especially people we believe are good hearted. The more obedient we are to God the more we become one of those people that our friends seek out for spiritual guidance. To be righteous is to pray and worship regularly.

Prayer: Jesus, on my own I have no hope of purifying my thoughts or of becoming righteous, but I know that with the help of the Holy Spirit, my thoughts, my words and my actions will become pleasing to God.

May 16

Jesus and his disciples went to the villages near the town
of Caesarea Philippi. As they were walking along, he
asked them, "What do the people say about me?"

Mark 8:27

Reflection: What did the people who saw Jesus in person think of Him? We have never seen Jesus in person and yet here we are putting our faith in him. We do so confidently because our conscience agrees with his teachings and with the way he lived. Even atheists like Richard Dworkin remarked that "Jesus is a great moral teacher." More importantly when we follow Jesus, we begin to experience things which bring wisdom and which bring us closer to the things we hear from our conscience. Jesus stands for peace, happiness and self-discipline. Jesus loves us so much that he gave up his life for us. Jesus came to teach us that the way back to God is through love. No other religious teacher speaks like Jesus did.

Prayer: Jesus thank you for teaching me good and life giving lessons and for atoning for my sins. May I always be privileged to call you my Lord and Master.

May 17

I lie down and sleep; I wake again for the Lord sustains me.

Psalm 3:5

Reflection: Even for people who do not believe in God, the biggest hope at night on going to bed, lies in waking up the next morning. This fact highlights the extent of our lack of control over some fundamental aspects of life. No one can guarantee tomorrow. But lack of control is no reason for us to have irrational beliefs or faith. Christianity is rational because it makes perfect sense and it delivers what it promises. Christianity teaches skills which enables us to get along well with each other and which helps us to reach our potential as spiritual beings. Unlike false religions which emphasize rituals or superstitions, our faith is a way of life in which love of others, and compassion, are paramount. Our faith calls us to examine what we do in light of the fact that our behavior can cause pain to other people. No teaching attributed to Jesus is controversial, and following Jesus' teachings has been shown to be most fulfilling. And so we believe that it is the Lord who sustains human life. When we appreciate God's might, our worries and fears diminish.

Prayer: Father, I know that all my fears arise from lack of faith and trust, help me to better reflect my faith in my daily activities.

May 18

All the paths of the Lord are steadfast love and faithfulness, for those who keep His covenant and His decrees.

Psalm 25:10

Reflection: God's covenant with us is that if we repent and accept the teachings of love and charity that Jesus brings, then the Holy Spirit will abide in us. As much as God loves us, like a good Father, He is not pleased when we dabble in sin. The business of sin is very serious. And no one can deny that there is a lot of pain and suffering in the world. Every sin opens a door to the devil who delights in bringing us pain and sorrow. Without God's steady hands, we are doomed to pursue selfish desires. In the end we find pain, misery and death. Everything we learn from God is for our good and the good of the world. To keep God's covenant is to lead a purposeful life.

Prayer: Spirit of God, help me to be faithful to the teachings of my Lord and Savior Jesus so that I may remain on the path of love and faithfulness, first with my family and friends and then with everyone I come across.

May 19

*You call me Teacher and Lord – and you are right, for
that is what I am. So if I, your Lord and teacher, have
washed your feet, you also ought to wash another's feet.*

John 13:14

Reflection: Foundations support the weight of structures above
them such as houses. Some of the people who rejected Jesus did so
because Jesus was not a king who wore a golden crown and sat on a
throne. Instead, He was born in a manger on a straw bed and later
was amongst outcasts and people of low status. Jesus hung around
people who acknowledged their shortcomings and wanted healing. By
washing the disciples' feet, Jesus showed that it is Godly to bear the
burden of others and to do so with humility. Jesus is the foundation
upon which humanity rests, and Jesus calls each Christian to lend a
shoulder for other people to lean on.

Prayer: Lord, help me to become an instrument of Your compassion
so that I may serve by lending a shoulder to those who are tired and
weary.

May 20

*And even the hairs of your head are all counted. So do
not be afraid; you are of more value than many sparrows.*
Matthew 10:30

Reflection: We are separated from God on account of our sinfulness.
But God has not stopped loving us or caring for us. God is all-loving
and all-powerful, and we should not expect anything less than a
complete knowledge of how His children are doing. We are not alone
in the world. We often feel that it is not right to bother God with little
things. This is not true. There are no little things in the sight of God. If
it is important to us, then it is important to God, no matter how trivial
we think the matter is. God is never too busy to hear from us. In fact,
God is most pleased when we delight in His company.

Prayer: Spirit of God, help build my faith so that I may be able to
turn to God for all things, small and big. Thank you for wanting to be
involved in all aspects of my life.

May 21

Give to the one who begs from you, and do not refuse the one who would borrow from you.

Matthew 5:42

Reflection: Needy people sometimes makes us feel guilty so we avoid their company. This is not necessary because we are all needy and God can provide sufficiently for everyone. God wants obedience from us and not sacrifice. What God asks of us is that we are there for each other so that the love and gifts we have received from the Lord are shared with others. A cornerstone of Christian faith is charity and Christians are renowned worldwide for charitable works which sometimes do not involve money. Mother Teresa served with no money and William Wilberforce, the English parliamentarian who was instrumental in ending slave trade in the civilized world, did so by taking a stance in the British Parliament. Blessings from those we assist far outweigh what we give them.

Prayer: Father thank you for all the gifts You have bestowed on me. May I always be open to sharing these gifts with other people.

May 22

Do not believe every spirit but test the spirits to see whether they are from God, for many false spirits have gone into the world.

1 John 4:1

Reflection: Anyone can claim to be a prophet. Every so often cults surface in the name of Jesus. Some of these cults even manage to convince their followers to commit acts of violence or suicide. People are rightfully skeptical when God is associated with violence, wars, intolerance, or racism. Actions that are not grounded in love or compassion, fall short of the teachings of Jesus and so, if we are ever in doubt about what we are told, love is the test that will reveal whether the teachings are from God. The Father is the source of all that is good and so any message from God is always good and peaceful.

Prayer: Lord, help me to build a pure desire for You so that I am never tempted by teachings which promote hate or which divide people. Today, I will carry Your message of love and forgiveness to all I come across.

May 23

Let your fountain be blessed, and rejoice in the wife of your youth, a lovely deer, a graceful doe. May her breasts satisfy you at all times; may you be intoxicated always by her love.

Proverbs 5:18-20

Reflection: Strong prayer! How we treat a spouse is often a good indicator of where we are in life. It is often through a spouse that we learn patience, gentleness, forgiveness, and how to love other people. If we can't learn to cherish the person we share a bed with, a person who cares about our welfare, then we will find it hard to love anyone else. A faithful marriage turns a schoolboy into a gentleman and a schoolgirl into a lady. Two is better than one, so let us work hard in building solid and nurturing relationships. If we keep our eyes away from other people, and we avoid tempting situations, then we will find it easier to remain in love with our spouse.

Prayer: Lord, help me always to focus my thoughts, my eyes, and my affection on the spouse you have given me so that we can grow old in each other's arms. Today, I will show my partner that I very much appreciate him/her in my life.

May 24

*...do not swear, either by heaven or by earth or by any
other oath, but let your "yes" be yes and your "no" be no,
so that you may not fall under condemnation.*

James 5:12

Reflection: Whether it is to God or to other people, we should reflect before we make promises and then we should endeavor to keep our promises, if at all possible. We often make promises to God in times of need but when things improve, we tend to walk away from our pledge. It is easy to become lazy when things are going great, but if we don't watch it, trouble soon resurfaces and we feel terrible that we were unfaithful to our promise to God. The solution is to stay close to God through thick or thin so we can keep moving forward. Likewise, when we make promises to other people that we are unable to keep, that turns us into liars. As far as other people are concerned, our problem sometimes is that we like to have it both ways. We are tempted to lie, to look good before others. But if we work hard doing what we promised, when we should, we need not lie. As God's people we must be seen as having integrity. We don't want to say one thing and do something else. When we break commitments to others, we are taking advantage of others by deceiving them; when we break a promise to God we are disappointing Him. Our word must always be our bond; both with God and with fellow humans.

Prayer: Lord, teach me integrity so that others can rely on my promise and so that I always take my pledge to You seriously. Today, I will endeavor to think before I make promises that I can't keep.

May 25

*The lazy person buries a hand in the dish, and is too tired
to bring it back to the mouth.*

Proverbs 26:15

Reflection: Laziness is a killer of talent. We owe it to each other to
work when we are able to and not to waste time. Time is precious.
When used properly, time brings lasting happiness and fulfilment.
We each have gifts that enrich the world and so we all lose when
one person fails to contribute her gifts. God gave us time to enjoy
our work. If we work hard and treat other people's business as we
would treat ours, we would find our work extremely satisfying. God
blesses good labor and rewards the laborer with sweet sleep. This verse
reminds us that there is purpose to our lives.

Prayer: Lord, may my hands never be idle, help me to enjoy providing
for myself and for my family. Today I will endeavor to be as diligent
as possible.

The Scriptures say, "God accepted Abraham because Abraham had faith in him." Money paid to workers isn't a gift; it is something they earn by working. But you cannot make God accept you because of something you do. God accepts sinners only because they have faith in him.

Romans 4:4

Reflection: This passage reminds us that there is no one who does good all the time. There is no one who abides in the Lord all the time. Indeed as we mature spiritually we realize that God is the author of any good that we have in us. And so there is no one who can say that God owes them this or that, in terms of reward for perfect obedience. It is by God's grace that we are sustained. God himself is the one who sets a path for our salvation. Our response to His call is not to swim against the tide of repentance, but to trust in the Lord as we let the tide carry us along.

Prayer: Father, I acknowledge that I have not always dealt fairly with others, and so I pray for everyone whom I have hurt in any way. Thank You for assuring me of Your forgiveness.

May 27

*Do not be quick to anger, for anger lodges in the bosom
of fools.*

Ecclesiastes 7:9

Reflection: Anger is about pride and revenge, it is about thinking we
deserve more than we have been given. We all get frustrated, but it is
not wise to let frustration lead us into anger or hate. Anger causes fat
to be deposited into our blood vessels and causes our blood pressure
to rise. The fat deposited remains unused and forms plaque, which
constricts and narrows our blood vessels and sometimes leads to
blockage. Exercise burns away fat and strengthens the heart muscle.
Many people are surprised that the Bible talks about such things, as
anger and pride. But these are two fundamental faults, and they are
often at the root of more damaging behaviors, such as interpersonal
violence and wars.

Prayer: Lord, let me always remember that I, too, frustrate others
sometimes with my behavior. Teach me patience and teach me
understanding so that any anger in me will be replaced with humor,
and not violence.

May 28

If you tell people that you belong to me, I will tell my Father in heaven that you are my followers. But if you reject me, I will tell my Father in heaven that you don't belong to me.

Matthew 10:32

Reflection: Faith is becoming an old fashioned word, especially amongst young people. Churches are empty. Yet we read daily that people in the world yearn to live in Western countries. Christian dominated countries are always ready to welcome refugees, in accordance with the teachings of Jesus, they are not hostile to strangers. And so it is a blessing to be born and raised on principles of peace and love that Jesus teaches. Instead of being ashamed to be called Christians we should focus on showing people that we love Jesus because He was a man of love and peace. And we should be weary of people who ferment trouble or people who promote hate against other faiths.

Prayer: Father I love your teachings because they make me better and because they help me understand the world. I pray that I will continue to strive at being a better person.

May 29

Can you understand the mysteries surrounding God all-powerful? They are higher than the heavens and deeper than the grave.

Job 11:7

Reflection: We are the most intelligent beings that God created and so we can be excused for thinking that we are capable of understanding God Himself. Imagine an ant trying to understand human existence. Impossible. The chasm is even greater between us and God, in terms of understanding God's existence. Yet, when we pay attention to the events in our lives and when we put our inner voice above all else, we see the handiworks of the Creator. God is nearer that we realize but we can know only what God reveals to us about Himself. We are creatures and so we are limited to what senses we have been given.

Prayer: Spirit of God, deepen my experience of faith and protect me from pride and arrogance so that I do not start to believe that I am capable of discovering all mysteries in life. Today, I will keep reminding myself that I am Your creation.

May 30

You claim to be innocent and argue that your beliefs are acceptable to God. But I wish He would speak and let you know that wisdom has many sides. You would then discover that God has punished you less than you deserve.

Job 11:4

Reflection: People who dwell on God day and night tell us that we feel only a fraction of what we deserve for the pain and havoc we create in the world. No one is innocent. When we feel the need to rationalize our action it is often because our conscience is uncomfortable with what we have done. We do this because it is important to us that we think of ourselves as good and decent. If God revealed to us the depths of our hearts, we would flee in despair. Mercifully, God shields us from ourselves and He gently helps us to address our shortcomings. In the above passage Job reminds us of God's mercy.

Prayer: Spirit of God, thank You for being so gentle with me and for granting me another day in which to learn how to be faithful to Jesus. I will remind myself all day of Your loving mercy.

May 31

---◦○◦---

Our Lord will punish anyone who doesn't know God and won't obey His message. Their punishment will be eternal destruction, and they will be kept far from the presence of our Lord and His glorious strength.

2 Thessalonians 1:9

Reflection: It is impossible to know God and to obey His message without repenting of past transgressions. Apostle Paul in this letter to the followers of Jesus is cautioning that we should not take God's grace for granted by persisting in wickedness. God has called us to a new life through repentance and it is up to us to accept or to decline God's call. No one can claim to be blameless because we all have an inner voice which tells us right from wrong. If we persistently ignore the gentle prodding of the Spirit inside us, then we stand the danger of being separated from God's love. The absence of God is hell.

Prayer: Lord, may I never appease my conscience by denying the Father. Help me to confront my wrongdoings so that I may not be separated from the Savior of the world. I pray that I will have the opportunity this day to show Your loving kindness to my friends and family.

June 1

Be not overly wicked, neither be a fool. Why should you die before your time?

Ecclesiastes 7:17

Reflection: Sometimes we think of God's teachings as arbitrary in that they have nothing to do with everyday living. This is not true. This passage is pointing out that wickedness and foolishness can bring on a lot of stress and that stress makes us appear older than we are. Stress brings on diseases and other issues which shorten life. Easily angered people are unpleasant to be around and this verse tells us that wickedness hurts our physical body. God gives us faith so we can let go of anxiety. Faith is trusting God with things that we cannot control.

Prayer: Father God, please help me to trust You and to learn to leave matters that I cannot control in Your loving and just hands. Help me, Lord, to stay healthy by learning not to be anxious, jealous or angry.

June 2

How great a forest is set ablaze by a small fire! And the
tongue is a fire.

James 3:5

Reflection: If Adolf Hitler was not such a fiery orator, perhaps he
would never have been able to persuade other people to support
his diabolical schemes. Hitler used his tongue to lure people into
wickedness. Our tongue is best used to build, but it is a difficult thing
to tame. Most of us are not accustomed to reflecting or pausing long
enough before we speak. And, even when we pause, we usually simmer
with a desire to get even or to put someone in their place. If we have
enough faith and enough love in us, we will be more willing to turn the
other cheek rather than to unleash the tongue on those we disagree
with. Better to use love to dampen a fire of hate than to use the tongue
to incite evil. Control of the tongue is something that should be on a
Christian's prayer list.

Prayer: Spirit of God, teach me to hold my tongue in check, and to
use the words that come out of my mouth to build, and not to destroy
others.

June 3

Incline your ear and hear my words and apply your mind to my teaching.

Proverbs 22:17

Reflection: The extent of human misery and despair should convince us all that there is something the matter with the choices we make. Children learn about wars, infidelity, favoritism, intolerance, and racism, from their parents. The Bible tells us that we are born into sin. But God has not abandoned us to sin. The amazing thing is that even when we reject God, our conscience still hounds us whenever we ignore it. It is interesting to note that psychiatrists have given up trying to rid humans of guilt. Most thinkers now accept that guilt is integral to our nature. The only antidote for guilt is forgiveness. Jesus came to show us the way, He led by example.

Prayer: Father, I know that practice makes perfect and so if I were to develop a habit of coming to You daily, I would be so much wiser and so much more content. Help me to put into practice the things that I know will help me become a better person.

June 4

The one who sows sparingly will also reap sparingly, and the one who sows bountifully will also reap bountifully.

2 Corinthians 9:6

Reflection: This is a verse that is often used by clergy and preachers to invite us to give money. The money to run churches has to come from somewhere. But sowing Jesus is not just about money, it is about being there for each other and about putting the effort in to be faithful to the teachings of Jesus. This verse challenges us to put our best foot forward, to use the talents that we have been given to the fullest. We are not judged by how much we sow but how much effort we put in. To whom much is given, much is expected, and so we can't all sow equally but we can each do our best with what we been blessed with. The harvest is plenty but most times the workers are few.

Prayer: Spirit of God, enable me to make the best use of my gifts. Help me to be a good witness to the people that I come across today.

June 5

No eyes have seen, ear has not heard, nor have entered into the heart of man, all that God has prepared for those who love him.

1 Corinthians 2:9

Reflection: Our senses make us appreciate life. But this life's possibilities are much more than any of us have experienced. Even in the face of the difficulties and learning that we all go through, we cling to life because it can be incredibly satisfying and stimulating. The Bible tells us that God has even greater things in store for those who answer His call. We can only imagine! How does one love God? We start by fulfilling our innate desire to be good, and by being obedient. Anyone who loves God is prepared to do things he would not normally do, like forgive his adversaries.

Prayer: Who is more worthy of my adoration than You, Father God? Grant that I may find lasting joy in You and that today I will show my love for You by doing all that You ask.

June 6

As I live, says the Lord, every knee shall bow to Me, every tongue shall give praise to God.

Romans 14:11

Reflection: Jesus is not a king that delights in seeing people bow and prostrate before him. Kneeling has always been a sign of respect and is still very common in traditional societies. To kneel before Jesus is to show appreciation for his sacrifice on our behalf. To kneel before Jesus is to respect the Word of God and to respect each other. To kneel before Jesus is to acknowledge that we are not deserving of God's mercy, but for Jesus' sacrifice. And so no one is more deserving of our respect, than the one who laid his life down for us. One day every tongue shall be delighted to give praise to God because God is good.

Prayer: Jesus, I will kneel before You as my true King and Redeemer. Remember me before your Father and grant that I may merit to be called Your servant by my actions today.

June 7

Because of the Lord's great love we are not consumed, for his compassions never fail. They are new every morning; great is your faithfulness.

Jeremiah 3:22-23

Reflection: Normally when a child does wrong he is corrected immediately. And so it is with us and God. We are admonished immediately after a wrong doing. (Next time you do wrong, pay attention to what happens immediately after.) But if we ignore the correction we may find that we have been given over to sin. And it may appear to us, as we persist in the sin that we are getting away with evil after all. This is a scary state because being given over to sin can mean that we actually experience the pain that sin brings directly. There is a difference between a fatherly correction and the pain of sin. The good news is that each morning provides us with fresh opportunity to repent and to return to God. God's love and compassion is so great that He is willing to forgive us no matter how late in the day we come to Him. A day spent apart from the Lord's guiding Spirit is a day of missed grace.

Prayer: Spirit of God, help me to never ignore your corrections. May my heart always be compliant and yielding to the way of Jesus.

June 8

When anxiety was great within me, your consolation brought me joy.

Psalm 94:19

Reflection: This passage reminds us that it does no good to think about sorrowful things. While it is true that there are enough things in the world to send anyone into despair, there are also many more things that are pleasant and that are worth dwelling on. One of the problems with negative thoughts is that they are too often exaggerated. People we think are suffering are usually not suffering as much as we think they are. We have a choice as to what we wish to think about – positive or negative thoughts. This is not to belittle the plight of those people who are clinically depressed and who require help from professionals. But aside from a clinical condition, there is no reason why we should allow our minds to dwell on negative things or on worries about tomorrow. To do so is to deliberately bring sorrow to oneself. This is a form of self-torture.

Prayer: Father, help me to delight in the beauty of the world around me particularly in the wonderful people in my life. May my thoughts be filled with wonderful delights and may I have a smile on my face all day today.

June 9

Do not overcome evil with evil, but overcome evil with good.

Romans 12:21

Reflection: People who swear to teach their enemies a lesson are overcoming evil with evil. We learn early that "two wrongs don't make a right." And so it is that we are to pray when we encounter evil, rather than seek to do evil. No evil will ever undo another evil. And it has been shown by psychologists that revenge is not fulfilling. Not only does it keep the wound open, it keeps the cycle of violence going (such as a continuing feud or vendetta between families, groups, or nations). Good, on the other hand is a great example to show our enemies. Christians must follow the example of Jesus, a man of peace and forgiveness.

Prayer: Father God, help me to always repay good with good and to do good even in the face of evil. Help me to pray for those that may wrong me today.

June 10

In everything I did, I showed you that by this kind of hard work we must help the weak, remembering the words the Lord Jesus Himself said: 'It is more blessed to give than to receive.'

Acts 20:35

Reflection: The life we have is a gift and all the things we cherish are gifts from God. Freely we have received, freely we should give, Paul tells us. There is only so much we need and there is only so much we can consume. Yet many of us are blessed well beyond our needs. How lucky we are then if we are in a position to give back some of what we have received from God to others. Who has not been the recipient of kindness? We, therefore, must not close the door on the needy who come knocking. It is not about who deserves our help; it is about who needs our help. Christians, following the example of Jesus, do not direct help only to other Christians but to whoever is needy.

Prayer: Thank You, Father, for all the people that You have brought into my life to help me become who I am today and thank You for the people who will come into my life in the future. May I too be there to help others as I have been helped.

June 11

I am the light of the world. Whoever follows me will never walk in darkness but will have the light of life.

John 8:12

Reflection: Jesus lit up the world with His teachings and by the way He lived. He paved a path of love for all those who wish to do the will of God. How fortunate we are! Not only do we have the laws of God written in our hearts, we also have the Holy Spirit which shines a light on the path laid out by Jesus. To walk the straight and narrow path is not about a prayer here and a prayer there; it is about acquiring self-knowledge and about recognizing the weakness of our humanity. We need a light to shine the way because we have walked so far away from God that many of us even deny His existence.

Prayer: Lord, thank You for being my light. I know of no one as gentle and as loving as You and I pray that I will always walk behind You. Today I will walk in the light of the Lord.

June 12

---⊸○⊸---

Truly I tell you, there is no one who has left house or brothers or sisters or mother or father or children or fields for My sake and for the sake of the good news, who will not receive a hundredfold now in this age.

Mark 10:29-30

Reflection: Sometimes we grow up with parents who are more interested in tradition than they are in spiritual truths. Christians do not necessarily follow the spiritual teachings of their parents, they follow Jesus. Our Christian faith came from Judaism, but when the followers of Jesus were denied a place in the synagogues, Christianity became a full-fledged religion separated from its Jewish roots. No one is born "Christian". People can only become a Christian by a voluntary decision to follow the teachings of Jesus and to be baptized. By long-standing tradition the Catholic and some other Churches baptize infants, but children are not in full communion with the Church, until they affirm their commitment at a later age, whereas many other Protestant Christian churches only baptize mature believers. Even then, the Church teaches that every person must seek a personal relationship with Jesus, our sole High Priest. In this sense, every Christian is a convert to the religion. People are not born as "Christians".

Prayer: Holy Spirit, help me to reflect the love of God to my friends and family so that those who are seeking You may see Your Son in me. I pray that every member of my family will accept You and be willing to put God ahead of traditions.

June 13

Do not join those who drink too much wine or gorge themselves on meat, for drunkards and gluttons become poor, and drowsiness clothes them in rags.

Proverbs 23:20

Reflection: How much we eat, how long we sleep, and how fit we are, may not seem to be matters that God cares about. But God does indeed care about all aspects of human life. If we eat too much too late at night, the digestive process keeps us from enjoying a deep sleep. If we develop a habit of sleeping in, then we waste the precious time we could be using doing valuable, spiritually edifying, and interesting things. Jesus said, that even the hair on our head is counted by God. The Father loves us and He knows us better than we know ourselves; and God demonstrates this love by His involvement in all aspects of our lives. People who are active and don't oversleep stay fit. These are the types of practical teachings we can expect when we study Jesus.

Prayer: Thank you, Father, for Your enduring love. Help me to take good care of my earthly body, I promise to stay active and agile today.

June 14

For it is by grace you have been saved, through faith –
and this is not from yourselves, it is the gift of God.

Ephesians 2:8

Reflection: Some people ridicule the idea that the sins of Adam and Eve brought pain into the world. But when our ancestors disobeyed God, their disobedience gave birth to our fleshly life, so to speak. But we too are just as disobedient as our ancestors were, and in this sense we are born into sin. All persons with a mature conscience are in need of God's grace and so our journey back to God is not the result of good work on our part. It is the result of a clemency which is available to all who, as Jesus said, seek to do the will of God. To be saved through faith is to strive for the fruits of the spirit: love, patience, compassion, forgiveness. From a spiritual point of view, one sin is enough to destroy life, and so it is entirely the result of Jesus' atonement and God's love that we now have hope. If Adam and Eve had remained obedient to God, they would not have become the parents of broken humanity and we would not know pain and suffering.

Prayer: Thank You Lord for atoning for the disobedience of Adam and Eve. Spirit of God, I confess that pure thoughts do not always go through my mind and I pray that You will help me to love others as I love myself. Make today the day that I think good things all day.

June 15

Do not let your hearts be troubled. Believe in God, believe also in me.

John 14:1

Reflection: Because we do not see God in a physical sense, it is easy to lose heart when things are rough. It is also easy to deny that life has any structure or purpose when we are in the midst of a crisis. As well whenever we decide to succumb to temptations, it is convenient to deny God and to claim that the voice of our conscience was put there by parents and teachers. But Christians have hope and we trust that troubles will never overwhelm us because God is always in control. From experience we know that troubles never last, and that we come out stronger at the end. This hope comes from our conscience which tells us that God accepts a contrite heart. It also comes from the fact when we act with love, all goes well, just as Jesus taught. Trouble is often a sign that we are straying, and so trouble should only make us yearn for God even more fervently. God is found whenever we open our heart to spiritual teachings.

Prayer: Lord, help me to always place my trust in You so that I may never give up hope of overcoming my troubles, especially when my heart is troubled. I pray that I will be able to demonstrate my faith in You today by not allowing my heart to be troubled, no matter what I encounter.

June 16

Whoever does not receive the kingdom of God as a child will never enter it.

Mark 10:15

Reflection: Our ancestors, whom the Book of Genesis refers to as Adam and Eve, God's first human creation, were taken by God as His children. But disobedience brought separation from God. Jesus now tells us to call God our Father because he has paid the price for this disobedience. We express our gratitude through how we treat one another and through trust in our Father. Children are not prone to worries or overthinking. Children enjoy the moment and do not go to bed worrying about tomorrow. Until we learn to trust in God we will continue to stress and to make bad decisions. Trust brings calm and a clear head. This is one of the points that Jesus is making in the above verse.

Prayer: Spirit of God, teach me to understand that I am a child of God so that I do not get lost in the traps of the evil one.

June 17

The Lord confides in those who fear Him; He makes His covenant known to them.

Psalm 25:14

Reflection: Despotic rulers do terrible things because they think there is no one on earth to hold them accountable for their actions. But even kings answer to God in their personal lives. Wise people fear God because they realize that how they treat other people is how life will treat them. God makes each one of us confront our choices. However, fear is not what symbolizes our relationship with the Father; love and forgiveness do. But a wise man can never forget that God is privy to all he does and that God alone can hold us fully accountable. To fear God then is to respect His teachings.

Prayer: Spirit of God, help me to always respect the laws of God, so that my heart will not yield to fear, except for the fear of my Creator. Today I will respect everyone I come across.

June 18

A gossip betrays a confidence, but a trustworthy person keeps a secret.

Proverbs 11:13

Reflection: We all say things that we do not wish repeated to other people, from time to time. This verse reminds us of our responsibility to pause before speaking especially if we are discussing other people. We must not betray confidences and destroy other people's character. No one enjoys being the subject of gossip or hearing someone repeat something told to him in private. Imagine being a fly on the wall and hearing people you have never met, discussing your character, or repeating things that you had told your friend. It is very hurtful to break a confidence and it makes others feel like we cannot be trusted. Even the writers of the Bible think so badly of gossip that they admonish those who do it. Our friends have every right to trust that we will not betray their confidences.

Prayer: Spirit of God, help me to guard my mouth so that I don't betray the confidence of those who trust me with their secrets. I promise that today, I will not say anything negative about anyone.

June 19

Put away your former way of life, your old self, corrupt and deluded by its lusts.

Ephesians 4:22

Reflection: Life is about choices and we have many models of life to aspire to. We can choose to do whatever feels good for the moment regardless of the consequences. Or we can choose to be concerned with the welfare of other people. Not all choices yield peace and lasting joy. Until we come to God with a contrite heart, life can be dull and full of haunting memories. There is a mirror directed at us at all times, even if we claim to have no spirituality. We become starkly aware of this mirror when we answer the call of God. As we walk towards God, we see some of the finer details of our shortcomings in the mirror. God's desire is that we will invite the Holy Spirit to change us into new beings. But we need to remember that such a change is ongoing and so we should be prepared to become disciplined by prayer.

Prayer: Spirit of God, help me so submit daily as You mold me into a purer being. I thank You Father for giving me a choice to live life as I wish. But I like Your teachings and so I pray that today You will be proud of my efforts in this regard.

June 20

Wine is a mocker and beer a brawler; whoever is led astray by them is not wise.

Proverbs 20:1

Reflection: A glass of wine with the evening meal can be satisfying. Watching a favourite program on television is invigorating. This simple verse cautions us against excesses in life. Too much of a good thing can be terrible. God has blessed us with a lot of things but the same items which can be joyful can also bring trouble, when we let them control us. A 15 minute break which turns into hours of computer gaming takes us away from good work. When a glass of wine becomes 3 or 4, we start to say and do silly things. When we are not in control over what we do, then the enemy usually is in control. Incidentally, in Biblical days, wine was usually not as potent or as strong as wine and other spirits of today.

Prayer: Father, thank you for wine and for the things I love doing. Help me to control these things so that they do not control me. Today, I will not allow anything negative to control me.

June 21

Children, obey your parents in the Lord, for this is right. Honor your father and mother which is the first commandment with a promise so that it may go well with you and that you may enjoy long life on the earth.

Ephesians 6:1-3

Reflection: Parents give up so much for their children. Even parents who could not afford to keep their children are still making a huge sacrifice out of love by giving them up for adoption. What parents want in return are happy children who love them. God assures us that if we honor our parents, then our children will, in turn, bring us joy and honor. Elderly parents become like young children in terms of their emotions and nothing brings them more joy than a visit from their children. One thing that we must remember is that the honor we give our parents should not depend on how good they were to us.

Prayer: Thank You for my parents and thank You for all the love and sacrifices they made on my behalf. Teach me to honor them so that they might always find joy in my presence. I forgive my parents for any mistakes they may have made while raising me.

June 22

Therefore I tell you, do not worry about your life, what
you will eat or about your body, what you will wear.

Luke 12:22

Reflection: This is not a call to be lazy! Hard work is good and it is
through work that we serve the world. This is why those who don't
work or volunteer often find life not as satisfying as those who put in a
day's work. There are of course people who are unable to work because
of disability, but those us who can work must do so. Jesus is telling us
in this verse that once we have done all we can, we must not worry
about matters beyond our control.

Prayer: Spirit of God, I know that worry shows a lack of trust in God,
teach me to trust in our Father in heaven and not to worry about
things beyond my control. Today I will not allow myself to worry
about things beyond my control.

June 23

Make me know Your ways, O Lord; Teach me Your paths.

Psalm 25:4

Reflection: People generally become more spiritual with age. The reason for this is that through experience we come to realize that there is a relationship between spiritual devotion and the quality of life. "Make me know Your ways, O Lord." This is a heartfelt prayer. When we say this prayer we are really begging God to be patient with us as the Holy Spirit uses life experiences to teach the truth to us. "I am the way, the truth and the light," Jesus said. We know this to be true because when we follow Jesus's teachings we acquire a greater capacity to love and we also grow in wisdom. The teachings of Jesus resonate with the spirit in our heart and so we recognize Him as the Christ of God. The way of God and the path of God are the attributes we see in Jesus. Next time you come across a gentle, kind and thoughtful person, consider that this is the type of person that God wishes for us all to become. Jesus was meek and humble.

Prayer: Father God, I cannot argue that Your way is goodness and love. Teach me to desire the goodness that Jesus exemplified with his life, so that today I may be able to say that I carried my cross behind Jesus.

June 24

God opposes the proud, but gives grace to the humble.

James 4:6

Reflection: Perhaps proud people attempt to cover up their insecurity with pride. To be proud is to look down on other people or to exploit the weaknesses of others. To be proud is to treat other people less than we would want to be treated. People who have wealth often think that economic or social success equals moral superiority. There are countries where people are assigned social status on the basis of skin color or gender, and there are (or were) even churches that assign responsibility on the basis of skin color. At the time of Jesus, religious hierarchy was more rigid than it is today, and people shunned other people on the basis of faith. This is pride before God, whereas humility is a sign of greatness before God. Humble people do not count themselves as superior to other people.

Prayer: Father, all that I am, all that I have, are the result of your grace. I have done nothing to deserve my family or my friends or even my place of origin. Today I will make myself accessible to everyone I come across.

June 25

Rid yourself, therefore, of all malice, and all guile, insincerity, envy, and all slander.

1 Peter 2:1

Reflection: Many parents are overjoyed when their children start learning about Jesus, especially as Jesus lived the way that He would like us to aspire to. Even people who are born into other faiths must admit that Christianity as taught by Jesus, calls for people to be at their very best. This verse tells us some of the negative things that we are called to fight against. Envy comes in many forms. If you knew that John your friend would not share the lottery jackpot with you, would you be happy if he won the big lottery, or would you rather that a stranger won? We often crave so much attention that we forget the needs of others. We are reminded in this passage that we must not let selfish desires cause us to wish other people bad or to sully their name.

Prayer: Father, I know not how I came to be full of things that I am not proud of, but I pray for assistance in cleaning out the envy and malice within me. Today I will wish everyone that I come across the best that life has to offer.

June 26

The Lord looks down from heaven on humankind to see
if there are any who are wise, who seek after God.

Psalm 14:2

Reflection: It is not possible to think of something more important than seeking after God. If we believe that God made this world, then we must believe that God is in control and that God is capable of meeting our needs and desires. To seek after God is not to abandon our earthly responsibilities which are a part of what it means to know God. To seek after God is to put God into everything that we do, so that our motives are always pure. No power can do more for us than God can, and so if we turn away from God it is because we are not wise. If we are lacking in wisdom, it is not because God has withheld wisdom from us. In fact, life is designed so that problems arising from the choices we make will point us in the right direction and we would gain wisdom. If everything went well for us, no matter what choices we made then we would never realize our mistakes. To seek after God is to seek after wisdom. To run away from God is to shun our best source of sustenance and love.

Prayer: Lord, I have shown with the choices in my life that I have a lot to learn about wisdom. Teach me your wisdom so that I may live life more fully and joyfully.

June 27

Those who are well have no need of a physician but those who are sick do.

Matthew 9:12

Reflection: Jesus said these words to people who claimed to be pure, people who criticized him for paying attention to the down and out. The Bible tells us that sin entered the world through Adam and that redemption came through another person, Jesus. Sin is a sickness and one of the symptoms of sin is that it turns us away from God. It makes us reject the idea that we are moral beings subject to moral judgment by God. Sin destabilizes us and causes trouble amongst friends and family. God chose not to abandon us to this sinful state and so we have Jesus, the great teacher and Redeemer and we have the Holy Spirit available to us day and night. Christians accept that we are broken people and are therefore in perpetual need of God's healing power.

Prayer: Father, my body hurts and my spirit grieves, heal me as only You can. For ever may I feel Your healing touch.

June 28

Rise from the dead and Christ will shine on you.

Ephesians 5:14

Reflection: To be separated from God is to perish. To rise from the dead is to realize the endless possibilities that Jesus offers us. Someone once said: "Every day may not always be good but there is good in every day." Without a spiritual awakening life becomes all about gratification of the flesh as we stumble from crisis to crisis, seeking pleasure. But a life of gratification soon becomes tiresome and too painful. It is only by coming to Jesus that the spirit within us begins to grow and become pre-eminent in our existence. While we are wearing a mortal body we are supposed to be dead to its desires so that conscience is always in control. We are dead and broken by sin, for all intents and purposes by the time we come to Jesus. But it is those people who are rebuilt that are best suited to minister to others.

Prayer: Lord, the more I know myself, the more I realize how much Your love sustains me. Use my life as You will. Today, let Your light shine on me and on my friends and family.

June 20

Everyone who believes that Jesus is the Christ has been born of God and everyone who loves the parent loves the child.

1 John 5:1

Reflection: To be born of God is to accept God's gift of redemption through His only begotten son, Jesus. Historians agree that Jesus lived about 2000 years ago. They also agree that Jesus was of exceptional character. The few other sources of Jesus' story confirm what we read in the New Testament – that Jesus did and said things that made Him unique amongst everyone that has ever lived. Jesus Himself challenged anyone who doubts His origin to seek the will of God. Jesus' point is that anyone who seeks after God, will discover the attributes of God in Jesus. It is impossible to love God and reject the love and forgiveness that Jesus stands for. If we wish to learn about his divinity: Was Jesus the Son of God? This is a simple question we can ask God.

Prayer: Father God, I acknowledge that faith is a gift which comes from you. I pray that my faith will empower me to live without fear.

June 30

A cheerful heart is good medicine, but a crushed spirit dries up the bones.

Proverb 17:22

Reflection: Laughing or being happy has been shown to produce chemicals that nourish life. As well, remaining joyful requires a positive attitude and this is contagious. When we are cheerful we tend to bring true joy to others, we light up their lives and we fulfill the wish of God. Ultimately, God wants people to be joyful and to be happy. On the other hand, being gloomy serves no purpose and helps no one. People avoid those who are negative, and so if we enjoy people, then we should cultivate a happy attitude. Rejoicing, this verse tells us, will make us live longer. This is God's wish for us.

Prayer: Father, please help me to focus on the great things in my life, so that I might be happy and content. I thank You, Father that You have given me so much to be happy about.

July 1 — Canada Day

Let mutual love continue. Do not neglect to show hospitality to strangers, for by doing that some have entertained angels without knowing it.

Hebrews 13:1-2

Reflection: The point of this verse by the apostle Paul is not to encourage us to do good for the sake of receiving a reward from angels. The point is to encourage us to cultivate a habit of doing good at all times. Good is worth doing for its own sake and because it brings joy to others. And if we all did good, then we will all derive joy from our interaction with one another. Paul's point is that our good deeds should not be selective, they should be offered to all people who need our help. And it is often strangers who are away from family and from friends who most need our help. Some people have the gift of charity and others have the gift of discipline. It is God that chose which gifts to bestow on us. Often God entrusts us with riches because God knows that we will remember the cry of the poor and needy. We should welcome every opportunity for charity as a gift from God.

Prayer: Father God, may I never regard anyone as a stranger. Help me to understand that it is a privilege to give, rather than to receive, especially to strangers who have no means of repaying me.

July 2

*For while we are still weak, at the right time Christ died
for the ungodly.*

Romans 5:6

Reflection: Today's sinner can become tomorrow's saint and today's
unbeliever may become another Apostle Paul. Because no one is born
into the faith, all Christians were once alien to the faith and without
salvation. To be ungodly is to behave in a manner that disregards the
welfare of other people. As descendants of Adam and Eve we inherit
their flesh. Everyone has sinned and so everyone needs the grace of
God. This passage is our reminder that there was a time when we were
outside God's call and Jesus died for us. And so those we consider
today to be outside of the faith are nonetheless still much loved by
God. As well, we need to remember that we are always weak in so far
as our ability to remain good is concerned. This is why even after we
are born again in the Spirit, we continue to stumble and will always
require the Holy Spirit by our side. The difference is that as children
of God, we do not return to the past, we move forward towards a
better future.

Prayer: Thank You, God, that in spite of my weakness and sinful
nature, You have chosen to redeem me. I pray that all people will come
to accept the teachings of Your Son Jesus.

July 3

Devote yourself to prayers, keeping alert in it with thanksgiving.

Colossians 4:2

Reflection: Changing one's life for the better comes quickly to those who are devoted to prayer. Jesus prayed all the time. We need prayer to keep us focused, especially when things start to go well. Happy times are when we tend to become careless and too sure of ourselves. And this is when, for most of us, we are liable to encounter fresh difficulties. The key to stopping complacency is to develop regular devotion. When we pray daily, we are less likely to forget our issues and we are more likely to stay alert in the face of temptations and less likely to return to old habits. Prayer for a Christian is daily medication for the soul.

Prayer: Father God, may I never forget how much Your Son prayed when He was here on earth. Today I will pray and glorify You in all that I do.

July 4 — National Holiday of the United States of America

For we know only in part but when the complete comes, the partial will come to an end.

1 Corinthians 13:9-10

Reflection: At best, each of us only sees a piece of the puzzle of life. But even prophets know only a small part of life's story. There is no one who is capable of completely understanding the mystery of God. Atheists are sure that they know what's going on in the world but with great respect to all ostensibly well-meaning atheists, anyone who thinks he knows everything is much mistaken. As maturity sets in we begin to realize how little we know and how much we take for granted. And the more time we spend pursuing goodness the more we become aware of how much our views were obstructed by the wrong choices we made in the past. And so it was that when the perfect image of God came as Jesus, people who thought they knew more than they did, rejected Him. They could find nothing immoral with Jesus' teachings, but it was sufficient that He challenged the status quo.

Prayer: Lord Jesus, daily I appreciate how perfect Your teachings are. I cannot find fault in the moral lessons You have passed on to us. May I never be separated from You.

July 3

O guard my life and deliver me; do not let me be put to shame, for I take refuge in You.

Psalm 25:20

Reflection: God alone knows our deepest fears and secrets and God alone can comfort us sufficiently to give us everlasting peace. What parent will shun a child who comes to them for refuge? So it is, that God will not let shame come to those who embrace His guidance. If we have doubts about God's loving grace, the chances are, we are struggling with our faith. One of the purposes of Jesus' life on Earth is to open the way for us to the Father. The Jewish tradition had been, that the priest spoke to God on our behalf, Jesus however, told us to call God our Father and to talk directly to God. The Lord is our refuge and strength.

Prayer: Father God, may I never be put to shame or slandered, and may I always be quick to build up people, and unwilling to attack their character. Today I will smile knowing that You are my refuge and strength.

July 6

Surely there is no one on earth so righteous as to do good without ever sinning.

Ecclesiastes 7:20

Reflection: The physical flesh that we wear, descended as it did from sin and disobedience makes it impossible for us on our own to live a pure life. This is a challenge to all of us to become more faithful to God's word. Righteousness is not about keeping rituals or about knowing the Bible inside and out. This verse does emphasize for us the significance of the sacrifice that Jesus made on our behalf. We owe our redemption to Jesus and to God's love for us. Even though our disobedience has brought us to the point of pain, God is here with us.

Prayer: Lord, I wish to do Your will. May You be able to say to me, "Well done, My good and faithful servant." Today I will rejoice knowing that what I cannot accomplish on my own has been accomplished for me by Jesus.

July 7

Whenever you stand praying, forgive, if you have anything against anyone; so that your Father in heaven may also forgive your trespasses.

Mark 11:25

Reflection: An unforgiving heart is a heart burdened and troubled. To forgive is to release the negative energy contained in anger. One of the teachings that set Jesus apart through the ages is that He taught forgiveness rather than revenge. He rejected the idea of an eye for an eye. Today forgiveness and rehabilitation is a cornerstone of civilization. God, as Jesus taught us, never calls upon people to take revenge on one another. Instead Jesus taught that we are to leave vengeance to God.

Prayer: Father forgive me of my wrongdoings, which are long and numerous, and help me to forgive others as well as to forgive myself.

July 8

For everything there is a season and a time for every matter under heaven.

Ecclesiastes 3:1

Reflection: Aside from the fact that repeating cycles help us to keep track of time, one reason that human life and the rest of the universe are cyclical, is because life is about constant renewal. A new day starts, a new week starts, a new month starts, a new year starts, we have a "birthday" every year. Also repeating cycles help us to better see the patterns around us and to learn new things. Renewal is a symbol of God's constant forgiveness. There is a time to play and a time to reflect. There is a lot to learn and the repeating seasons help us in grasping life's lessons. Spirituality is not meant to be a millstone around our neck; true spirituality deepens our capacity to enjoy life, to laugh more, and to appreciate the environment around us. There is a time to laugh, a time to work hard, a time to visit the sick, a time to pray for prisoners, and a time to worship the Father. If spirituality is causing us sorrow, then there is something wrong with our approach.

Prayer: Father, help me to make good use of the precious time I have been given. I thank You for the repeating opportunities, that You provide for me to make amends for past mistakes.

July 9

You shall be holy, for I am holy.

1st Peter 1:16

Reflection: God's work is not complete in us until we, his children, are no longer willing to succumb to temptations or wickedness. We can only exist with God as holy and blameless. To be holy requires repentance. Repentance means that we remain open to the Holy Spirit as the Spirit gently reveals to us our inner self. Our thoughts, words and actions, must all be subjected to spiritual control as we march towards the purity of heart which will enable us to see the loving God. This is God's target for us.

Prayer: May I never vex the Holy Spirit and may my soul be open and yielding to the prodding of Your Spirit, Lord, so that I may be holy and have a place in Your mansion.

July 10

And we know that in all things, God works for the good of those who love Him, who have been called according to His purpose.

Romans 8:28

Reflection: God's love, much like the love of a parent for a child, is unconditional. But imagine how much more God delights in those who love Him with all their hearts. While it is only human to expect that our commitment to a spiritual awakening should bring lasting and immediate joy, we need to remember that a spiritual walk is actually like a school where we learn the ropes over time. It is in this spiritual walk that we learn discipline and devotion, we learn what it's like to suffer through mistakes, and we learn to feel pain, so that we, in turn, can minister to others. But our experiences are not undeserved or unbearable. The Spirit merely uses our own experience to help us to better appreciate the plight of others. God uses everything for good. So even the bad that we do, teaches us empathy for our own good. There are no coincidences in life, all things work for the good of those seeking goodness.

Prayer: Father, thank You for counting me worthy to be called by You. May I respond to Your love today, by loving You with all my heart and all my soul.

July 11

> *But we all with unveiled face reflecting as a mirror the*
> *glory of the Lord, are transformed into the same image*
> *from glory to glory, even as from the Lord the Spirit.*
>
> 2 Corinthians 3:18

Reflection: Children reflect the nature of their parents and Jesus, the son of God, reflected the attributes of His Father. And so, if we claim to be children of God, we too should reflect God's attributes so that people we meet will think about God when they meet us. We are blessed with faith and wisdom so that our relationship with others can be built on love. People who follow Jesus' teachings learn forgiveness and sow peace. The more time we spend with the Lord the quicker we will be transformed into an image that glorifies God.

Prayer: Lord, help to carry my cross daily so that I may serve others diligently and so that others may be reminded of You when they meet me.

July 12

Then Jesus said to his host, "When you give a luncheon or dinner, do not invite your friends, your brothers or sisters, your relatives, or your rich neighbors; if you do, they may invite you back and so you will be repaid. But when you give a banquet, invite the poor, the crippled, the lame, the blind, and you will be blessed. Although they cannot repay you, you will be repaid at the resurrection of the righteous."

Luke 14:12-14

Reflection: From the human point of view, there are few things worse than ingratitude. But a wise person does not expect a payback for doing good deeds. Our payback is the good itself. But this is the way it should be. We receive favors, we pass on favors, and this good keeps on going forever like chain letters. If we are generous to those around us then we will have lots of people wishing us well. After all, we are called to be servants, and servants work with no expectation of gratitude. This verse reminds us that it is unwise to be eager to receive favors, and slow to return favors or to pass favors on to others.

Prayer: Spirit of God, help me to show gratitude for the kindness I receive and may I show kindness to all those I come across. I pray for all those people who have said kind things to me and who have been generous with their time, or with other gifts.

July 13

I bless the Lord who gives me counsel; in the night also my heart instructs me.

Psalm 16:7

Reflection: What do we want from God? We want good health, wisdom, happiness, fulfillment, great family life, forgiveness of sins, etc. And so we seek guidance from God, as to what, if anything, we can do to advance our case so we can have the things we want. Sometimes we think it is selfish to ask God for things. This is not true. Jesus reminded us that we have not because we ask not. If we heed the counsel of God all things shall be added unto us. So if we desire lots, we must be prepared to heed the teachings of Jesus so we can become wise.

Prayer: Lord, Your counsel delivers me from evil and guides me towards life. Help me to abide in You so that I will always bring my questions to You.

July 14

If you love me, you will keep my commandments. And I will ask the Father, and He will give you another advocate to be with you forever.

John 14:15

Reflection: If we keep Jesus' commandments, we reap the benefits of a more fulfilling life. But another incentive for striving for good behavior, is to express our appreciation for Jesus' sacrifice. This means that when we don't feel like doing something because of pride or just stubbornness, we do it anyway, because of Jesus. The good news is that whenever we desire to do God's will we can always count on help from the Holy Spirit. On our own we are liable to remain stubborn and inflexible. The disciples were very fearful and timid until they received the Holy Spirit. After this they were able to heal others and to perform miracles.

Prayer: Father God, stir in me a yearning to love You, to please You, and to yield to Your Spirit of love. May Your Holy Spirit be my constant companion so that I may always be able to express my gratitude to Jesus.

July 15

But no human being can tame the tongue. It is a restless evil, full of deadly poison.

James 3:8

Reflection: One of the hardest things to do is to tame the tongue. After we have learned that it is wrong to strike at other people, we often continue to use our tongue as a means of extracting revenge. The fact is that what we say to other people often reveals a lot about us. And the tongue can cause as much damage as physical force. We have all read about people who take their lives because others make fun of them. It is not everything that occurs to us that bears repeating. With social media now it is much easier to do harm by spreading nasty things about others. If no one listens to or reads bad news, then no one would bother to spread it.

Prayer: Holy Spirit, please give me strength so that I may never say negative things about others and so that I may never delight in reading or listening to negative things about other people.

July 16

I also said to myself, "As for humans, God tests them so that they may see that they are like the animals".

Ecclesiastes 3:18

Reflection: God does not test us in the sense that God throws obstacles or temptations our way to see how we would react. When we draw closer to God, we become more aware of our faults so that together with the Holy Spirit we can overcome them. The saying that the Lord disciplines those He loves means that God exposes us to our faults and this is why it often seems like God is testing us. The difficulties we encounter in life are of our own doing, God merely allows us to confront them as need be. As we draw close, we may realize that doing wrong bothers us more than before, this is a good thing. This is progress.

Prayer: Father, keep me from despair as I discover new things about myself. May your peace and joy propel me, each day and help me to learn from my past mistakes.

July 17

God is spirit, and those who worship Him must worship in spirit and truth.

John 4:24

Reflection: It is interesting that Jesus' concern for human life had to do with how we use the free will that God gave us. Jesus is concerned about morality. This is what true religion is about – learning to love people. God is the perfect example of love. God is good and pure, thus, no evil can stand before the Spirit of God. The Spirit of God and the Spirit within us are not subject to time or space limitations, like our physical body. Time ravages our body but we are made to grow in spiritual dominance as the physical body breaks down. To worship God in spirit and truth is to reject all selfish desires of the flesh, anger and pride. To worship God in spirit is to walk behind Jesus and to put the love of God above all else.

Prayer: Spirit of God, I pray that You will nourish the spirit within me so that any desire or habit which does not glorify God's Holy name will be extinguished.

July 18

This God – His way is perfect; the promise of the Lord proves true; He is a shield for all who take refuge in Him.

Psalm 18:30

Reflection: A shield is an armor which protects soldiers from swords or from spears thrown at them. The word of God acts as a shield against the temptations of sin. And so, to take refuge in God, is to abide in Him and to trust in His promise. The enemy of God is likewise our enemy, day and night he labors to devise new tricks to trap us with. Jesus proved that God's way is perfect. None of his accusers could touch Him until He was ready for them. The best thing we can do then is to start the day by reading God's word and talking to God. This is the shield that will protect us all day long.

Prayer: Holy Spirit, may Your light shine into my heart and may Your loving mercy preserve me, so that today all manner of evil will flee from me.

July 19

Who then is the faithful and wise slave whom his master has put in charge of his household?

Matthew 24:45

Reflection: We read that Joseph, a slave, rose to become the second most powerful person in Egypt. Moses was also born into slavery, yet he found favor with God. Many African slaves brought to the New World embraced the teachings of Jesus wholeheartedly and their descendants remain some of the most fervent Christians today. God has called everyone to His banquet but those who accept and act on the invitation are the faithful wise slaves. However, those who hear God's call, but remain unmoved, continue to be slaves to sin. If we use our time for the benefit of each other, then maybe we too can be that faithful slave, whom Jesus refers to. Life is given to us freely by God. But because all is not well with our world, we each have a role in the creative process. We have the option to give back our time to God, by serving each other.

Prayer: Lord, kindle in me a love for God that is never extinguished. Upon Your return, may You find me hard at work in Your vineyard.

July 20

———◦◦———

Drink from it, all of you; for this is my blood of the covenant, which is poured out for many for the forgiveness of sins.

Matthew 26:27

Reflection: Symbols are often used to drive home a point. The bowl that Jesus ate the Last Supper in, is known as the 'Holy Grail' and is the focus of many stories about Jesus. The cup that Jesus shared with the disciples emphasized the Lord's sacrifice on behalf of humanity. Since then, churches around the world offer bread, wine or juice as Communion and every time we partake in this ritual, we incorporate the body and blood of the Risen Lord. To some people, this is a strange practice. To us, it is a good way to keep fresh the memory of Jesus and what Jesus means to us.

Prayer: Lord, give me the water of life so that I may never be thirsty and the bread of life so that I may never be hungry. May Your body and blood renew me daily.

July 21

God's kindness is meant to lead you to repentance.

Romans 2:4

Reflection: Jesus tells a story similar to this: The owner of a vineyard went out to hire workers. The first worker was delighted to receive a thousand dollars for ten hours of work because this was higher than the going rate. Every hour until midnight, the owner kept bringing in workers and paying each a thousand dollars. When the first worker discovered that he had been paid the same as the last worker, he became unhappy. But why should he be unhappy, after all he was paid more than the going rate and he had agreed to the pay. Jesus told this story to illustrate how envious we can be. After all, the generosity to one worker did not take away anything from the other workers. God's kindness is shown by His patience. God waits and waits for us to return to Him and we should be glad and not envious that God is kind to all, even to those who come into the fold, last minute.

Prayer: Father, thank You for Your grace. May I respond to Your patience with a contrite heart and an eager spirit. Today I will not envy my neighbor.

July 22

Today if you hear His voice, do not harden your hearts.
Hebrews 3:7

Reflection: Every day we hear God's voice calling us to Him. But what would God be calling us to do? God is calling to show us what is required and that we can do better. God invites us to a closer walk with Him. God wants to teach us more about who we are and show us how many of the choices we make cause nothing but headaches for us and for those around us. God calls us to use the gifts and the talents unique to us for the betterment of each other. We are created in the image of God, and the voice within us speaks to the Holy Spirit, so even the very wicked is redeemable and is called by God. Jesus welcomes a murderer on the cross with him into paradise, demonstrating that there is hope for everyone who answers God's call. To harden one's heart is to reject the grace of God and to refuse to grow spiritually.

Prayer: Father God, here I am to do Your will. Mold me as only You can so that I can better serve Your purpose. Today, I will answer Your call, my God.

July 23

If I have all faith, so as to remove mountains, but do not
have love, I am nothing.

1 Corinthians 13:2

Reflection: What good is our faith unless it motivates us to act
for the good of others? If our faith causes us to be hateful or to be
disrespectful to other people, then this is not a faith worth having.
There is no easier way to turn people away from God than to engage
in hate, discrimination, or to act without compassion. We often hear
people on television advocating views which appear to contradict
the teachings of Jesus. Instinctively, we are either skeptical of these
views or we conclude that they are not true "Christian" views. This
is because we know that to be Christian is to strive to reflect the
attributes of Jesus. God is about love, gentleness and forgiveness. The
Christian faith is not about prayers and fasts, it is primarily about how
we treat people.

Prayer: Father God, may I never bring You shame as Your child. Help
me to deepen my faith in Your promise and in the teachings of Your
son Jesus. Today I will practice my faith by showing love to everyone
I come across.

July 24

For your name's sake, O Lord, pardon my guilt, for it is great.

Psalm 25:11

Reflection: Humanists and atheists claim that the ideas of sin and guilt are terrible things that our puritanical society created to control people. This argument fails to recognize the fact that people, including atheists, hurt one another and that if we don't experience guilt for our wrongful actions then we will behave like animals with no internal compass to point us in the right direction. Everyone has done wrong in the sense that everyone is guilty of deliberately acting less than charitably, but those who acknowledge this fact and repent are further ahead than those who insist that morality is for weak minded persons. Wise is the person who realizes his weakness and is willing to accept the grace offered by God. Our feelings of guilt are what remind us that all is not well and that we should turn to God for mercy. The good news is that God will never reject a repentant heart. Unlike Jesus, humanists offer no guidelines on how we can improve human behavior.

Prayer: Father God, help me so that I may never deny my sins before You. May Your Holy Spirit help me to always move forward and never return to my former state of disobedience.

July 25

There is no one who is righteous, not even one who seeks God.

Romans 3:10

Reflection: God's kindness and grace lets us enjoy so much in this world that we forget that much more is possible. It is sad but true that we are more interested in ourselves than we are in God. We come to God because God calls each one of us by name. We come to God with problems and when the problems are solved, we are often nowhere to be found. And yet whenever we make any sustained effort to seek God, the peace and happiness we experience is unlike any joy that we normally have. If we fall short of the glory of God it is not because God has failed it is because our creation continues to evolve. Jesus was a man of prayer and we as Christians must seek to emulate him.

Prayer: Father God, I wish to love You with all of my heart and soul. Thank You God for Your everlasting love, and thank You for the gift of the Holy Spirit. Today I will seek God in all that comes my way.

July 26

I say walk by the Spirit and you will not gratify the
desires of the flesh.

Galatians 5:16

Reflection: To walk by the spirit is to stay focused on the teachings
of Jesus. People who live disciplined and spiritual lives tell us that
the more we live in the Spirit, the more we realize our shortcomings.
The flesh is not our enemy, it is a part of who we are on this earth. But
the main purpose of the flesh is to train us so that we will appreciate
good from evil. The flesh is all about giving pleasure to the body and
about taking advantage of others as animals do, but the spirit is about
doing good and looking out for people. Through this conflict between
the spirit and the body we come to appreciate the meaning of evil. If
we choose the spirit over flesh, then we confirm that we are God's
children.

Prayer: Lord, thank You for the opportunity that You have given me
to rise above my animal nature and to live in good will with other
people.

July 27

---

*The grass withers and the flower falls but the word of the
Lord endures forever.*

1 Peter 1:24-25

Reflection: Matter, including the human body is constantly changing
form. The word of the Lord is love and this never changes. We would
all like to live eternally with joy and with God. The physical body by
itself is not capable of living forever. But, though generations come,
generations go, the spirit of God endures forever along with the people
that Jesus has won over. Wickedness destroys human life, while
righteousness and wisdom lifts the heart and sustains life. Addictions
of all type - drugs, alcohol, sex, or anger - are often the result of a
troubled heart or an idle life. When we are using our talents well, we
will have less craving for bad habits. It is difficult to find peace until
we forgive ourselves and it is difficult to find meaning in life outside
of God.

Prayer: Lord, May the Spirit of the Father, sustain me and help me to
never take my prayers for granted. Help me to forgive myself.

July 28

The fruit of the Spirit is love, joy, peace, patience, kindness, and self-control.

Galatians 5:22

Reflection: Anyone that has perfect love, joy, peace and perfect self-control, perhaps has no need of much else. But those of us that are still growing know how much we need the help of the Holy Spirit. We are often told that we do not need God to be good. But on our own we are rough and gruff. It is only when we come to God that the spirit within us begins to yearn for love, joy, patience, kindness and self-control. This is because the mortal flesh we wear is subject to the rules of the jungle, survival of the fittest, in terms of brute force and cunning, and it is tamed only by spiritual desires. Our ancestors roamed the forests as uncultured savages, but through forgiveness we are received as children again, to be civilized by God's grace; to live in a world where people do not kill each other in war and where children do not die from starvation and diseases. As spiritual beings our goal is for a life of love and self-control.

Prayer: Father God, I know that I am one of Your highest creations. Help me to live in a manner that is cultured and loving. I know that hidden in plain sight are teachings about love, joy, peace, patience, and self-control. Today, help me to make the most out of all my experiences.

July 29

"For I know the plans I have for you," declares the Lord, "plans to prosper you and not to harm you, plans to give you hope and a future".

Jeremiah 29:11

Reflection: Atheists can be excused for having a gloomy attitude about life. After all if there is no God then there is no spiritual help and there is no hope of a better tomorrow other than wishful thinking. But for people who believe in God, life has a purpose and God has a plan for each life. God's plan is to help us become better people through insights and through learning from our mistakes. There is no shortage of resources with God and so we know that even when individuals and populations appear to be in dire straits, the Holy Spirit is with them and that their apparent difficulties are a part of God's plan of salvation. Some of the happiest people have very little. God's plan for all of us is to give us a most joyful life. But as many of us know, it takes a mature mind to remain humble and joyful when success arrives. Our challenge then is to learn life's lessons so that we can better appreciate the goodness of the Lord. We would have everything we ask for if only we could put them to good use and so the more we want from life, the more we must discipline our actions.

Prayer: Father, I know that there is a worthy lesson in all my troubles. Help me to better appreciate the simple things in life and to find contentment in Jesus.

July 30

⎯⎯◦◦⎯⎯

You are the salt of the earth, but if salt has lost its taste,
how can its saltiness be restored?

Matthew 5:13

Reflection: If we believe in our heart that God is love and that Jesus is His only son, then this is evidence that our soul has been touched by the Holy Spirit, and as Jesus said those who believe in him are no longer slaves but children of God. If then God is our Father we must reflect His attributes to those we come across, so that they will be reminded of God. He has called each one of us to work with him and those who answer the call of God become foot soldiers for the Holy Spirit. When we respond to God's call, we go through a form of schooling which cleanses us and teaches us wisdom and empathy. As we progress in this school, we too become teachers, ministers, friends, and companions and above all servants. Salt adds flavor to food and so we too are to flavor the world with love and service.

Prayer: Spirit of God, never cease to remind me that my lessons will never end until I am face to face with my Savior. May I never lose my saltiness and become useless in God's kingdom.

July 31

Blessed are the pure in heart for they will see God.

Matthew 5:8

Reflection: To be pure in heart is our ultimate goal which only the Holy Spirit can bring about. To be pure in heart means that we have no room for negative thoughts and that our actions are motivated by love. The road to this pureness starts with making our heart available to the teachings of the Lord. When we do so, we receive daily correction regarding our choices. The Spirit of God gently reveals our faults so we can understand their roots and renounce them. We may need to forgive those who have hurt us and created some of the anger we feel. There will be times when we feel disappointed about who we are, but this is progress and we should never be discouraged. We will emerge at the end of the journey with a pure love of God.

Prayer: Spirit of God, search my heart and my soul and help me to do away with all manner of wickedness including envy and hypocrisy. Help me so that I am able to keep going as You make me into a new person.

August 1

———◦◦———

When I look at Your heavens, the work of Your fingers,
the moon and the stars that you have established; what
are human beings that You are mindful of them?

Psalm 8:3

Reflection: The more that scientists are able to gaze into the universe, the more impossible it seems to them that life does not exist anywhere else but on Earth. Yet, despite countless numbers of inquiries life has not been found elsewhere. But what does it matter even if there is bacteria life in space? The verse above calls our attention to the fact that we are a tiny speck in the scheme of things. It also reminds us that we alone are made in the image of God, created for the sole purpose of reflecting the attributes of our maker. We alone have a spirit within us and so we alone share a self-conscious reality. Jesus told us that every strand of hair on our heads is known to God.

Prayer: Father, I have done nothing to deserve the gifts You have given me and I have done nothing to deserve life. Help me to show my gratitude for Your love by my obedience to Your commandments.

August 2

Do not be misled: "Bad company corrupts good character."

1 Corinthians 15:33

Reflection: If we roam the streets with a dog constantly, we will begin to do things that dogs do. There is a natural desire in each of us to be just like those around us and this desire is so strong that we would go against what we believe, if need be, just to blend with other people. As well, if we see something bad being done over and over, after a while, we become desensitized and don't see it as bad. The opposite is also true. If we see good things being done, we tend to imitate it. So good company helps us to become better. And so, if you do not want to end up like the people around you, then it is time to find new friends. You should seek the company of people you consider to be wise and you too will become wise.

Prayer: Spirit of God, build my character so that I can be a good influence to those I come across. Help me to be strong enough to walk away from the bad habits of other people.

August 3

Who gives speech to mortals? Who makes them mute or deaf, seeing or blind? Is it not I the Lord?

Exodus 4:11

Reflection: We have to account for what we do to each other. And we account to God. One of the statements in the Bible is that the fear of the Lord is the beginning of wisdom. But fear does not mean that God is arbitrary. Our relationship with God is about love and God's interest in correcting is so that we can learn love and goodness. Nonetheless the God that has the universe in the palm of His hand is awesome, to be respected and to be feared. God is the source of all that we hold dear and God is able to make our dreams come true.

Prayer: Father God, there is no one like You, no one who loves and forgives like You. I thank You for the senses You have given me and I pray for those who are without these senses, that their lives may be just as fulfilling and joyful.

August 4

---∘∘⊂---

Give thanks to the Lord for His steadfast love endures forever.

2 Chronicles 20:21

Reflection: It is too bad that it often takes adversity to help us appreciate the many gifts that we are blessed with. It is a very good idea to form a habit of regularly going over the things that we appreciate in life. This way we will not dwell enviously on the things we wished we had. If we can spend enough time doing this, then we will have little or no time left to feel sorry for ourselves. If we visited everyone we should visit, and return every phone call, our sleep will be so much sweeter. Trusting in God, trusting in the steadfast love of God and giving thanks for the new opportunities that God provides, is a habit worth cultivating.

Prayer: Spirit of God, help me to appreciate the gifts that God has given me. Thank You, God, for putting me in this world and I am sorry that I have not always focused on my blessings.

August 5

What then shall we say in response to this? If God is for us, who can be against us?

Romans 8:31

Reflection: God is always on the side of the righteous and this is one reason why revenge is always wrong. "Vengeance is mine," says the Lord. God makes everyone account for every unrepentant deed. Recently in the Middle East, a pilot involved in a bombing raid was captured and burned to death by his captors. The country where the pilot came from retaliated by hanging two prisoners and by sending in more pilots to bomb the enemy. The result is that more people died including an aid worker. This is an example of the cycle of death that vengeance creates in many parts of the world. We must pray that those involved in war will always respect human life.

Prayer: Lord I pray that those involved in war will always respect life, especially the lives of innocent civilians I know what pain and sorrow feels like and so I pray that I never become an instrument of pain for the innocent.

August 6

Good and upright is the Lord; therefore, he instructs sinners in the way.

Psalm 25:8

Reflection: We adore Jesus because of his goodness. We worship Jesus because he taught love, forgiveness and peace. People often deny God for various reasons. But even then, it is impossible to deny the fairness of God's laws written in our hearts. Many people who wandered away from God and tried to do things 'their way', often came back to God, acknowledging God's loving kindness and justice. Whenever we are willing to face up to who we are in terms of our moral behavior, we can't help but attest to the mercy of God. There is nothing that we have that God needs. We come to God to learn love and wisdom.

Prayer: Father, thank You for being so gentle as You instruct me in Your ways. Teach me to be just as gentle with other people.

August 7

And whoever would be first among you must be slave of all. For even the Son of Man came not to be served but to serve, and to give His life as a ransom for many.

Mark 10:44-45

Reflection: Those who faithfully try to follow Jesus say that it is impossible to truly follow God's commandments unless we first learn humility. The more we grow in wisdom, the more eager we are to bear each other's burden. The people we remember with fondness are those who have served humanity – such as Mother Teresa, Elizabeth Fry, John Bosco, and John Paul II. If God has put us in a position where we have much to offer, then we should be counting our blessings and rolling up our sleeves and going to work. Besides, it is better to serve, than to be the one being served. By following the examples of Jesus, great people put out their shoulders for others to stand on.

Prayer: Lord, teach me to follow Your example so that I too may wash the feet of my brothers and sisters. Help me Lord to serve faithfully and humbly.

August 8

Everyone who does evil hates the light, and will not come into the light for fear that their deeds will be exposed.

John 3:20

Reflection: Our human flesh knows evil, and knows good, and has the choice to do either. Animals behave as we do, but because they do not have our level of moral awareness, they are not judged by God as we are. Evil occurs when humans who should know better behave as animals. The flesh is made to perish, and so animals perish. But because we are both animal and spirit we have a chance to live like God; a chance to rise from the dead, as Jesus did. God is a God of love in that He is merciful and gives us much more than we deserve. But God is also a God of correction and so He helps us learn from our bad deeds. Who are those who do not fear the Lord? They are people who regularly ignore their conscience, who rationalize the hurt they cause to others. And so rather than remaining humble, they consider sin to be a myth, and they do as they please so long as human laws do not catch up to them. God is patient and so we're each touched daily by God's grace, so we may come to fear and shun wrongdoings. God does not ignore those who bring hurt to other people.

Prayer: Grant this, O Lord that my heart will tremble whenever I contemplate a wrongdoing; may my desire today be to live according to Your rules. Help me, O God, to live as your saints do, so that my flesh will not submit to animal drives, for my spirit yearns for life, not death.

August 9

Your beauty should not come from outward adornment, such as elaborate hairstyles and the wearing of gold jewelry or fine clothes. Rather, it should be that of your inner self, the unfading beauty of a gentle and quiet spirit, which is of great worth in God's sight.

1 Peter 3:3-4

Reflection: We can all be excused for wanting to appear as attractive as possible. After all it is well established that people favor those who look attractive. In fact, we should strive to be fit and active, and we should try to be clean and tidy in our appearance. And there is nothing wrong in trying to be fashionable or attractive so long as we do not become immoral or become obsessed with our appearance to the detriment of other things in life. But if all we have is physical beauty then we need to work harder at acquiring spiritual beauty. Outward beauty by itself is not that satisfying. We all know many beautiful people who are unhappy; moreover, physical beauty will fade. What is more lasting is the inner beauty that comes from a good, loving, and compassionate heart.

Prayer: Lord, I acknowledge that my desire to be favored by other people often drives me to worry more about my outward appearance than my inner beauty, help me to feel more secure and help me to put my spiritual growth above all things. Today I will treat people equally regardless of their outward appearance.

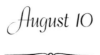

August 10

Watch and pray so that you will not fall into temptation.
The spirit is willing, but the body is weak.

Matthew 26:41

Reflection: Without spiritual direction the body is subject to the same drives we find in dogs and in other animals. When the spirit is relegated to the sideline, then the flesh reigns supreme. The flesh, as we all know, can be a source of short term pleasure and long term pain. If we are to rise above animal drives, then the spirit within us must take a prominent place. We can make that happen through living as Jesus taught. The teachings of Jesus will help us overcome the animal inside each one of us.

Prayer: Jesus, as a man, You conquered sin. I pray that I too will put in the effort to pray and to yield to the Holy Spirit so that my life might glorify my God.

August 11

Since we are receiving a kingdom that cannot be shaken. Let us give thanks, by which we offer to God an acceptable worship with reverence and awe.

Hebrews 12:28

Reflection: It is truly amazing to think that one day, perhaps soon, Jesus will be with us. The Kingdom that he will restore will have no end and it cannot be shaken by anyone. Until then we can more fully enjoy life if we follow Jesus' teachings. If we were invited to stay in a king's palace we would go out of our way to show respect by being civil and by obeying the house rules. We have now received an invitation to stay permanently in God's Kingdom and so we are being washed and cleansed, and taught the rules of the Kingdom. We worship God firstly by respecting God's laws and by respecting each other and the environment. We can show gratitude to God for all He does by learning humility and thanksgiving.

Prayer: Father God, I thank You for making a place for me in Your Kingdom. I am so sorry that I have often disrespected You by the way I behave. Help me so that I will never bring shame to Your Kingdom.

August 12

---⌗---

Blessed is that servant whom his master will find at work when he arrives.

Luke 12:43

Reflection: Even the toughest master will take kindly to a servant that is always hard at work. Our work as part of creation involves learning discipline, praying and meditating on the teachings of Jesus, and offering our time and resources as we are able to, for the benefit of each other. But unlike servants who toil for the benefit of greedy masters, what we do is entirely for our benefit and in return we receive the blessings that only children deserve. In this passage Jesus is inviting us to become dedicated to the task that God began in each of us. We are invited to carry our cross and follow Jesus.

Prayer: Spirit of God, help me to pray as many times as I eat daily so that I may continue to do my part in salvation and in building Your kingdom.

August 13

---◦◦◦---

The law of the Lord is perfect, reviving the soul; the decrees of the Lord are sure, making wise the simple.

Psalm 19:7

Reflection: The proof of the pudding is in the eating, so the saying goes. If God's law is perfect, then it should bring us joy and contentment. When we compare the results of living life on our own terms, with the result of living life according to the directions of the spirit within us, we realize how nourishing and perfect the laws of God are. It is only God's power that keeps us humble and kind to those we don't like. It is God's laws that make us strive to become better. And so one way to know whether we are following the rules of God is by considering how much peace there is in our life. There is nothing negative in God's teachings.

Prayer: Lord, may Your law revive my soul and make me wise. Today I will follow the decrees of the Lord.

August 14

Whatever you ask for in prayer with faith, you will receive.

Matthew 21:22

Reflection: When we pray in faith we are praying with a clear conscience. This does not mean that we are perfect, it simply means that we have dealt with those things that the Holy Spirit has revealed to us and that we are not praying for something hurtful. Even then, prayers sometimes do not show immediate results and so delay of time can make us feel as if God is not answering. The fact is that God hears all prayers but some prayers require a change in attitude from us and this process may take time as God, through the Holy Spirit, works to teach and to cleanse us. We are not robots, and so the process of prayer often requires effort in us as well. The Lord in this verse is assuring us that God hears prayers.

Prayer: Spirit of God, teach me patience so that I do not become too anxious or lose hope as You work daily to bring about changes in me.

August 13

---◦◦◦---

And the prayer of faith will save the one who is sick, and the Lord will raise him up. And if he has committed sin, he will be forgiven

James 5:15

Reflection: This is the type of verse that brings tears to one's eyes. It highlights the depth of God's love for us. There are reasons why we fall ill. Whatever the source of our illness, our Father cares to discuss it with us. What type of prayer do we utter to the Lord when we are ill or in trouble? Is it God's anger that brought us illness? Is the illness a part of God's plan for us or for those around us? Is it something we ate? Are we deficient in vitamins and minerals? The first thing we should do in illness is pray and seek help of professional people. Prayer will help us understand whether there is a spiritual connection to our illness and if this is not the case, we should still pray knowing that God is able to cure us or to direct us to those who could help us. The same God that gave us His spirit also made our body and as Jesus demonstrated several times, God has control over the physical body as well as our spirit.

Prayer: Father, please teach me about all the hidden things in my heart so that I will know myself and know the things which bring me pain. Help me to always understand any lessons that pain has to teach me.

August 16

Blessed are those who hunger and thirst for righteousness, for they will be filled.

Matthew 5:6

Reflection: To hunger and thirst for righteousness is to reject the transgressions of our youth and to yearn for wisdom. As we get older, we come to know our hearts well and we become more aware of how our behavior measures up or fails to measure up to our conscience. When we look in the mirror and are not entirely happy with all that we see, God desires that we invite the Holy Spirit, to come in and to help us into a new life. However, changing ourselves for the better is not a passive process; hard work and effort is required from us. We should be prepared to cultivate regular praying time as we confront our shortcomings. Even our thoughts need to be made pure.

Prayer: Spirit of God, create in me a deep hunger for goodness. Help me to walk closely with my Lord and Master, Jesus.

August 17

*I am the bread of life. Whoever comes to Me will never be
hungry and whoever believes in Me will never be thirsty.*
John 6:35

Reflection: Food nourishes the body. The Word of God nourishes the
spirit. The heart that strays from God is always restless and empty. We
are made to find fulfillment in the company of the Holy Spirit and so
when we go off doing our own thing, all that results is addiction, guilt,
and emptiness. There is no peace outside of the goodness that only
the Lord offers. Those who have walked with Jesus say that nothing
is more captivating and satisfying than travelling in the company of
the Holy Spirit.

Prayer: Jesus, may I continue to drink out of Your well, so that my
soul may find fulfilment and be satisfied. Today I will eat Your bread
and drink from the cup which gives life.

August 18

---◦○◦---

Do not merely listen to the Word and so deceive yourselves. Do what it says.

James 1:22

Reflection: What good is it if we read about the teachings of Jesus but fail to apply them to daily living? This was the problem that Jesus had with many of the religious leaders in His time. They were good at quoting Scriptures but poor at applying them. We saw this demonstrated in the story of the Good Samaritan. Jesus was a hard worker. We expect the lessons we teach our children to show up in their behavior. What God wants is that we too will put in the effort to absorb the teachings of Jesus. God's word has one purpose: to lead us to salvation and to enable us to live in peace and harmony with each other. There is a lot to learn but a mere ten minutes daily can make the difference.

Prayer: Spirit of God, teach me to be a doer of the Word like Jesus and not merely a hearer. I pray that I will continue to put in great effort at practicing what Jesus taught, even if I end up being persecuted for His Name like Stephen and the many who came after him, even to this day.

August 19

Once you were not a people, but now you are God's people; once you had not received mercy, but now you have received mercy.

1 Peter 2:10

Reflection: There was a time when almost everyone in the world worshipped sticks and stones and the sun. Ancient Egyptians even worshipped the Pharaoh as a god. Ancient Israelites on the other hand were led by prophets who taught them about the God who enabled a very aged woman, Sarah to conceive and give birth to a son Isaac. The point of this verse is to remind us that there was a time when we ignored God's outstretched arms, calling us to Him. We are the children who were kicked out of the house as a result of bad behavior. While we were out in the cold, God briefly allowed us to experience some of the consequences of our disobedience. But the gates that were once shut have now been reopened. Jesus died for us all while we were still sinners.

Prayer: Spirit of God, help me to find my way back to the gates that were once closed to me. I pray that I too, like Your servant Abraham, will put all my faith in You.

August 20

Whoever wants to be first must be last of all and servant of all.

Mark 9:35

Reflection: A servant is at our beck and call. From God's perspective a great man is a man who serves other people as a servant of the people. Servants do not expect to be respected and often do not get respect. In fact servants are rarely appreciated, they are more likely to be abused. God prepares us well, before we enter His service. Once we demonstrate a desire to learn, to love, and to grow. Service involves working with people in difficult situations, so people who work with them must learn patience and a non-judgmental attitude. This means that even when we think that someone is "undeserving" of help, we still owe the person respect and we can never forget that only God knows who is "deserving". God decides, and we obey.

Prayer: Holy Spirit, help me to never judge those that You send me to serve. Instead, deepen my empathy so that I may serve them with love and joy.

August 21

But since we are of the day, let us be sober, having put on the breastplate of faith and love, and as a helmet, the hope of salvation

1 Thessalonians 5: 8

Reflection: The image that emerges from this verse is that of a person going into battle. The passage is meant to remind us that daily we too are in battle. Evil is a force that must be overcome with a greater force. If it was so easy to choose good with all the temptation around us then there would not be so much pain on earth. We are in a serious battle for our very lives. The devil waits for the slightest misstep and bang, there is trouble. We put on the armor of God when we get on our knees at the beginning of the day, to pray and to ask for God's help. Our enemy never comes at us directly in a manner that is obvious. Instead, he is full of tricks to catch us off-guard. If we are surrounded by like-minded people, then we can watch out for one another, and make it that much more difficult for the devil to have his way with us. If we constantly worship God, that makes the devil flee! It is also said, "speak the truth and let the devil be afraid"!

Prayer: Father, from head to toe, You know me better than I know myself. Please cover me daily with Your love and give me an abundance of faith and hope to overcome the tricks of the evil one.

August 22

Wisdom makes one's face shine, and the hardness of
one's countenance is changed.

Ecclesiastes 8:1

Reflection: Wise people put their hope in God and worry less. Wise
people laugh more, trust more, and are more relaxed. Wise people
learn not to worry about things outside of their control and wise
people touch base with God daily. Wisdom, the Bible tells us, comes
from God to those who listen and to those who accept it. Notice the
hard faces of grumpy people and the fact that grumpy people tend to
focus on negative things. So another reason to smile, aside from the
fact that a smiling face is inviting, is that smiles make the face look
good.

Prayer: Father, teach me the type of wisdom which will keep joy in
my heart and a smile on my face, all day. Help me to brighten the faces
of those I meet today.

August 23

Anyone who resolves to do the will of God will know whether the teaching is from God or whether I am speaking on my own.

John 7:17

Reflection: What does it mean to do the will of God? And how does doing the will of God help us to understand who Jesus is? If resolving to do the will of God leads to an understanding of Jesus, then why are there different faiths? There are questions that we can take to God. The will of God is that we learn how to love so we can become pure at heart. Jesus was all about love and compassion so it is easy to connect Jesus with God. What we don't want to do is treat religion as a competition of cultures, with most people simply taking on the religion of their ancestors, even when the tenets of the religion make little sense.

Prayer: Father God, please unite all Your children and may the Holy Spirit guide everyone back to You. May Your Holy Spirit guide and protect those who are seeking You.

August 24

We are justified by faith, we have peace with God through our Lord Jesus.

Romans 4:13

Reflection: One of the hardest thing for a repentant soul to do is to forgive oneself. It is a lot easier to accept forgiveness from God; this fact should make us weary of sin. Eventually, it is our faith in the goodness of the Lord, which enables us to accept forgiveness and to be able to move on. On the other hand those who are without faith tend to rationalize their wickedness. We see then that God gives us faith not just to ease our mind regarding the unknown and the future, but also to ease our guilt and shame.

Prayer: Father God, thank You for the faith which enables me to forgive myself and which enables me to look forward to a better future.

August 25

Pursue peace with everyone, and the holiness without which no one will see the Lord.

Hebrews 12:14

Reflection: Attainment of peace often means that all sides must compromise. Having enemies creates anxiety, sleeplessness, and it curtails our freedom! The more enemies we have, the less free we are to come and go, and the less at ease we are. Plus, the way we treat our enemies, makes it easier for others to treat us in the same way. One way to minimize the number of enemies we have is to do our best not to take advantage of the weakness in our adversaries. The Christian way is to do what Jesus would do whenever we are in disagreement with other people. When we find ourselves in a position of physical strength, it is important that we do not act as bullies and give people reason to wish us bad. Life is more joyful for us when those around us feel well-treated and respected. Jesus our Savior was all about peaceful coexistence.

Prayer: Spirit of God, may I never unjustly bring pain and sorrow to others. Help me to understand it is never Your wish that I take advantage of other people's weaknesses.

August 26

Whoever is faithful in very little is also faithful in much.

Luke 16:10

Reflection: School children who learn the alphabet soon progress to the works of Shakespeare. Likewise, if we are faithful in the small tasks that God puts in front of us, we too can progress to bigger challenges. When the Apostles first came to Jesus all they could do was follow him around and watch him work. Later on the same Apostles were healing the sick and forgiving sins. We do not need to know all the secrets of life before we become devoted to spiritual growth. If we do the things we are certain of, then we will understand more mysteries of life. A phone call to a troubled friend, a hospital visit to an ailing aunt, are examples of things that will bring us so much satisfaction and cause us to go around looking for opportunities to do more.

Prayer: Spirit of God, help me to make the best use of my talents for the benefit of others. Help me to be diligent in all aspects of my life so that I may be fortunate enough to be given more tasks in Your vineyard.

August 27

There is one God; there is also one mediator between God and humankind.

1 Timothy 2:5

Reflection: Atheists and pagans ask why there has to be only one God and not many gods. By definition, God is the source of all things. There is not one god who made stones and rock, and another god who made trees and humans. The Hebrew prophets spoke of one God, Yahweh, the source of life. Jesus preached about the same God, his Father, the God of Abraham. We too proclaim this God because Jesus' teachings match perfectly the indelible laws in our heart. As well, our lives show that the Grace that He declared delivers us from the grasp of sin. No philosopher has fathomed a law more appealing to the human spirit, than that first proclaimed by the prophet Isaiah, and then by Jesus – love the Lord your God with all your heart and soul, and love your fellow human as yourself. There is either a God or there is not. If we believe in one God, there is no room for tarot cards, superstitions, horoscopes or divinations. There is no spiritual power in tea leaves or in stones and sand. We are to trust in God while doing the best that we can. Each morning, we should pray to God so we may focus on the tasks ahead of us. Jesus is our mediator because He experienced life as a human and died bearing our sins on his shoulder.

Prayer: I believe in One God, the Father Almighty and in Jesus Christ my Lord. Father, help me to learn from the wisest and most loving man that ever lived, Jesus. Help me so that irrational fears do not lead me to have irrational beliefs.

August 28

Charm is deceptive, and beauty is fleeting; but a woman who fears the Lord is to be praised.

Proverb 31:30

Reflection: Charm is often what we use to curry favor from other people. Charm is also what con-artists use to dupe their victims. Beauty is desirable but it will fade and so neither beauty nor charm brings lasting joy or salvation. The point of the passage is that we should not confuse charm or beauty with integrity. There is an argument to be made that the reason many marriages fail is because we put too much emphasis on charm and beauty. It is more profitable to put our effort into cleaning the heart, than in painting the face or seeking vanity. Beauty is good, charm can be good, but Godliness trumps them both.

Prayer: Father, lead me not into temptation and deliver me from evil. I pray that Your Holy Spirit will teach me to appreciate the beauty in Your creatures.

August 20

Love is patient; Love is kind; Love is not envious or
boastful or arrogant or rude.

1Corinthians 13:4

Reflection: During the initial period after we fall in love, we can
tolerate just about anything in our lover, and we would be willing to
do just about anything to make that person happy. Sometimes, this
attitude changes too quickly as the novelty wears off. Love comes
naturally to all of us, and what God wants is for us to always treat
other people with the same respect we show a new lover. Patience,
kindness and humility are attributes of love. In a healthy relationship,
partners bear with one another, never trying to outdo each other. In
fact, our spouse or partner is the one that is best able to teach us about
love. As we age and lose our physical vigor, it is love which helps to us
cherish the spouse or partner who has aged with us. A famous poet
wrote: "Grow old along with me, the best is yet to be!" So very apt,
and so true.

Prayer: Father, help me realize that my spouse is the best person to
teach me love and many other virtues. May the happiness we brought
each other in the beginning remain with us forever.

August 30

---•◦•---

For this reason, the mind that is set on the flesh is hostile to God.

Romans 8:7

Reflection: Animals are largely governed by drives and instincts. Animal behavior is like a reflex action, and so it is rigid, and sometimes even fixed. To behave like an animal is to ignore the moral consequences of what we do. A mind set on gratifying the flesh is constantly rationalizing his behavior so as to silence his conscience. The biggest rationalization for the unbelieving mind is that there is no God, or that God is only concerned with rituals. When we tell ourselves that there is no God, then it doesn't matter what we do or whom we hurt, since we do not believe in spiritual consequences. And so people who wish to live as they please are hostile to God, and the teachings of Jesus.

Prayer: Father, help me to accept that I am a moral being and that my behavior is to be guided by good will and not by animal drives and instincts. Today I will not set my mind on the flesh.

August 31

Religion that pleases God the Father must be pure and spotless. You must help needy orphans and widows and not let this world make you evil. Christians must look after those who are helpless.

James 1:27

Reflection: A famous man (Marx) once said that religion is the opium of the people. He is wrong. True religion is about learning to understand human nature so that our animal drives can be subject to spiritual control. Jesus is about love and compassion and about teaching us to be responsible beings. True religion makes us brothers and sisters, it does not divide us. All of the virtues that humanists claim that they want are the same ones that Jesus taught. The Christian religion demands that we work hard and enjoy life to the fullest so long as it is not at other people's expense. Religion that pleases God does not cloud our thinking like opium does, it keeps us sober so that we can discharge our responsibilities to one another.

Prayer: Lord, may I never require street drugs or alcohol to take my pain away. Help me to always understand the source of my pain and to be willing to allow the Holy Spirit to minister to my spirit.

September 1

Let us love one another because love is God; everyone who loves is born of God and knows God. Whoever does not love does not know God, for God is love.

1 John 4:7

Reflection: Anyone can preach about God and about love and anyone who is literate can quote Scriptures, but it is made clear by Jesus that anyone who does not love other people does not know God. We often hear people accuse other people of not behaving like a "Christian". This is because even those who are not Christians have heard of Jesus and know that Jesus is about love. Most of us are not very kind or very loving until we come to know God. This is because at the top of the teachings of the Holy Spirit is Love. If we had more love in our world, there would be fewer wars and more joy. Love is incompatible with violence.

Prayer: Father, I pray that everything I say or do will be motivated by my love for other people. Help me to recognize any hidden agenda within me, so that I might set it aside in favor of Your agenda for me.

September 2

In every place of worship, I want men to pray with holy hands lifted up to God, free from anger and controversy. And when you stand praying, if you hold anything against anyone, forgive him, so that your Father in heaven may forgive you your sins and pray.

1 Timothy 2:8

Reflection: One of the great benefits of prayer is that it is difficult to pray from the heart while continuing to nurse a grudge, hate, or anger against someone. Whether we like it or not, the more we pray, the more our minds remind us of our own shortcomings that require our attention. Prayer on a regular basis is very therapeutic and essential for self-knowledge and growth. The more we pray the more we learn to forgive and the happier we are. The most sobering thing we can do to start the day is to pray.

Prayer: Forgive me my failings, Lord, and help me to forgive myself and to forgive others. May I take more opportunities to get on my knees in prayer.

September 3

---

*Truly, I tell you, the tax collectors and the prostitutes are
going into the kingdom of God ahead of you.*
Matthew 21:31

Reflection: We sometimes find comfort in the idea that some group
of people are terrible sinners, worse than we are. But, unlike people,
God is not swayed by outward appearances or by the work that we do
or the title that we have. To whom much is given, much is expected,
and so we know that God takes much more into account than what is
apparent to us. The truth of the matter is that we all fall short of the
glory of God and so no one is better than the other. And Jesus captures
this fact by letting the religious leaders of His day know that many of
the people they consider to be terrible sinners may in fact be better
suited than they were, to receive the grace of God.

Prayer: Father God, help me to always remember that I am adopted
as Your child by grace, and that I am no more deserving of Your grace
than anyone else.

September 4

Do not let sins exercise dominion in your mortal bodies,
to make you obey their passions.

Romans 6:12

Reflection: There is nothing wrong with pleasure, indeed we are made to seek happiness. Many things, good and bad, excite the pleasure area of the brain. If we form a habit of stimulating the brain with things which bring us pleasure but destroy our body, or destroy friendships and families, then we invite trouble. Pleasurable habits are not easily broken. This is what the verse means when it talks of sin exercising dominion over us. Sinful habits are a great force to reckon with. The good news is that many good things are also capable of bringing us pleasure as well. Examples include work well done, charity, and many of the things we did as young children are still there; walking outdoors, playing in the park, sports, these are pleasurable events. Thank God that Jesus broke the yoke of sin, and so sin no longer has dominion over us.

Prayer: Spirit of God, help me to replace all unhealthy and destructive pleasures in my life with those that will build up good character in me and keep me in good health. Today, with Your help, Holy Spirit, I will turn my back on a bad habit for good.

September 3

———◦———

For we are his workmanship, created in Christ Jesus for good works, which God prepared beforehand, that we should walk in them.

Ephesians 2:10

Reflection: We all know, or have heard about an elderly person who continues to serve humanity with joy and vigor. Many of these people will tell you that nothing is more motivating than knowing that their service is needed. When we make our lives available to the Lord, we can be sure that we need not worry about motivation or about energy. The needs of those we minister to will invigorate us. There are of course people who profess no faith but are out there offering themselves to others. This can be a good thing but with faith comes greater meaning and a sense of responsibility and a direction from the Holy Spirit. For those who hope in the Lord, or for those who serve others, there will be no exhaustion or lasting weariness.

Prayer: Father, I pray that You renew my body and soul continuously so that I may always find the desire and strength to serve other people. Today I will renew my strength in the Lord.

September 6

Whatever you do in word or deed, do all in the name of the Lord Jesus, giving thanks through Him to God the Father

Colossians 3:17

Reflection: Few things annoy us more than seeing a person we have helped being ungrateful. We hold the door open for someone and there is no 'thank you'. We give money to a relative, there is no 'thank you'; instead, the response is a plea for more. But Jesus tells us that we should neither expect nor receive accolades for our charitable works. When we help someone, the best attitude is to regard the good deed itself as its own reward. We are never to demand or expect gratitude and our willingness to assist is to be based on who is needy and not who we think is "deserving". Every opportunity to give is an opportunity to give thanks to God who has given us more that we need or deserve. If you have the means to give, then you should be thankful that it is not you who is needy.

Prayer: Father, freely I received Your grace and freely I must pass it on. Help me to give without expecting anything in return. Today I will give thanks for every opportunity that comes my way to bless people around me.

September 7

---◦◦◦---

With toil and labor, we worked night and day, so that we might not burden any of you.

1 Thessalonians 2:9

Reflection: We know that it is better to be the one giving than the one receiving. And so diligence is always a good thing. If we all do our share of work, there will be more than enough for everyone to eat. But when our hands are slack, we stand a danger of burdening others. And so this passage tells us that if we are capable of working, and if we have work to do, then we must work as sign of self-respect and a sign of respect to other people who may feel obligated to look after us. The sick, the disadvantaged amongst us must of course be well-cared for when they are unable to provide for themselves.

Prayer: Father, grant that I may serve, rather than be served. Grant that I may assist those who are unable to work due to sickness or disability, with a joyful heart.

September 8

---

*Come to me all you that are weary and are carrying
heavy burdens, and I will give you rest.*

Matthew 11:28

Reflection: A life which has no spiritual purpose is tiresome and
weary. Such a life has no faith or hope to renew it when the going gets
tough. We all want to do it on our own, to live as we see fit. But this
means that we will have to make up our own rule book. Compared to
God's rule book, a non-spiritual life brings more pain and sorrow and
the progress to a better life is slow. When we do it God's way we do not
have guilt to weigh us down because we know that Jesus has borne our
sins, and our strength is renewed regularly by the Holy Spirit. There
is rest in knowing that our sins are forgiven.

Prayer: Lord, thank You for carrying my heavy load. May my soul and
desire be renewed constantly by the Holy Spirit of God. Help me to
keep my commitment to live a more spiritual life.

September 9

I will put my laws in their hearts, and I will write them on their minds.

Hebrews 10:16

Reflection: None of us alive today met Jesus in person. And there are millions of people around the world who have never read a Bible or heard of Jesus. But we are still accountable for our actions because God's laws are written in the human heart. We know that the teachings of Jesus, come from the Father, because the Holy Spirit kindles these words in every heart. This is why even those who have never read the Bible or heard the name of Jesus spoken, know good from bad. Despite many gallant attempts, no one has found the means to do away with guilt, as part of the human experience. This shows that guilt is at the core of what it means to be human.

Prayer: Spirit of God, may I never try do away with the laws You have written in my heart. Instead may I reflect on these laws, all the days of my life.

September 10

The Lord is my shepherd, I shall not want.

Psalm 23:1

Reflection: Sheep eat and drink what the shepherd provides. They never really know what lurks around the corner. We too are vulnerable in that we have no control over much of life. The Lord is our shepherd and He has instilled life instructions in our hearts. In addition Jesus came and lived as one of us to demonstrate Gods love for us and to fulfill many Hebrew prophesies. And so even when things are rough we know that the Lord is always at hand and that our pain will lead us to greater awareness.

Prayer: Jesus, You are my shepherd and *You* alone restore my soul. May all my needs and wants be met in You, by Your teachings and by the guidance of the Holy Spirit.

September 11

---◦◦◦---

Do not let your heart envy sinners, but always be zealous for the fear of the Lord.

Proverbs 23:17

Reflection: We often assume that some people are so lucky that they get away with things, if it seems that way it is because God's time is not our time. The fact is that no one gets away with anything. Sooner or later everyone must come to terms with who he is. And so as we move on from darkness that is sin, into light that is life, the above verse tells us not to envy those that were left behind. If anything, we should pray for them and hope they follow our example so that they do not have to learn through pain. September eleven was the day that the Twin Towers in New York were destroyed by hijacked planes. Over three thousand innocent people perished. Unfortunately this mass murder which should have united the world in love has made people more fearful of each other and caused many more deaths.

Prayer: Father, may I always seek to follow those who treasure Your ways, and may Your Holy Spirit keep me from being distracted by those who seek to live care free without regard for the feelings of other people.

September 12

---

*He suffered and endured great pain for us, but we
thought His suffering was punishment from God.*

Isaiah 53:4

Reflection: Thousands of years before Jesus walked the earth, the
Hebrew prophet Isaiah spoke about Him as the One from God.
Many people saw that Jesus was indeed the Messiah even though
Jesus did not live in a palace and died in agony on the cross. This is
the mystery of God – that it was necessary for Jesus to atone for the
sins of humanity with His life. A blameless man put on the cross like
a common criminal by those He came to save! But thank God that as
a result of Jesus's suffering our own suffering and pain are alleviated.
Jesus forgave and prayed for those who hurt him and so we too must
forgive those who hurt us.

Prayer: Thank You so much, Jesus, for freeing me from the bondage
of sin. Thank You for giving up Your life for me and for my children
and their children. Today I will pray for all those who do not yet
acknowledge your goodness.

September 13

--- око---

For all that is in the world, the lust of the flesh, and the lust of the eyes, and the pride of life, is not of the Father, but is of the world.

1 John 2:16

Reflection: If a good and loving God made the world, how can there be something the matter with it? The answer is that God did create the world in one form or another, but humans have perverted and damaged the world. God made us co-creators but we brought pride, lust, pollution, and many painful things to the table. But just as there are people who damage the world, we are all called to make it better. Our task as Christians is to be the hands of the Holy Spirit, and to make the world a better place for those who come after us.

Prayer: Spirit of God, help me to become one of those who make other people better and who make the world a better place. Today I will ensure that my actions are pleasing to You, my Father God.

September 14

Someone gave a great dinner and invited many. At the
time for the dinner, he sent his servant to say to those who
have been invited, "Come; for everything is ready now."
But they all alike, began to make excuses.

Luke 14:16-18

Reflection: Many of us would be jubilant if we received an invitation
to attend the coronation of the Queen. Accepting such an invitation
would be a sign of goodwill towards her. The man who gave the great
dinner in the passage above thought he was inviting friends and well-
wishers. But envy and jealousy caused many of them to decline his
invitation. And so instead of having those he thought were his friends
at his banquet the man brought beggars and strangers. Jesus came first
to those around Him and many of them heeded His call. Through
Jesus, God has invited every person to His banquet, so that we can
all indulge in the fine food and wine, first laid out for the children of
God's initial promise.

Prayer: Spirit of God, may I hear my name being called to the great
banquet and may I respond with joy and enthusiasm.

September 15

---

*A sower went out to sow. And as he sowed, some seed fell
on the path, and the birds came and ate it up. Other seed
fell on rocky ground, where it did not have much soil,
and it sprang up quickly, since it had no depth of soil.
And when the sun rose, it was scorched; and since it had
no root, it withered away. Other seed fell among thorns,
and the thorns grew up and choked it and it yielded no
grain. Other seed fell into good soil and brought forth
grain growing up and increasing and yielding thirty and
sixty and a hundred fold.*

Mark 4:3-8

Reflection: Jesus' story highlights the fact that sometimes we are
not ready to bear fruit after we receive God's Word. Those who bear
fruit are the ones who put in the effort to grow what they learn. Faith
without works is dead. Christianity is about putting into practice on
a daily basis the teachings of Jesus. Unless we are prepared to build
on what we receive, we will not yield much fruit.

Prayer: Jesus, I wish to yield much grain for Your Kingdom. Help
me to lead a disciplined life so that I may put in the effort to live as a
Christian should.

September 10

I said in my heart, "Come now, I will test you with pleasure; enjoy yourself." But behold, this also was vanity.

Ecclesiastes 2:1

Reflection: A Yoruba proverb states: "Sorrow doesn't kill, reckless joy does". One of the hardest things for people to cope with is endless joy. Sustained joy can make us complacent, it can make us feel like we have arrived and nothing can go wrong. Once we become successful we begin to abandon the good things which brought us success. Evil thrives whenever we are too relaxed or whenever we are sure of ourselves. This is why Jesus taught that we are to remain watchful and to never abandon prayer. If we want to continue to be happy then we have to keep doing what brought us to the happy place. Indeed, God wants us to rejoice and be glad, doing things which do not harm the welfare of other people.

Prayer: Father, help me to handle love and joy in my life with humility and by abiding in You so that I never become boastful. Today I will be glad in doing things which glorify Your Holy Name.

September 17

---—◦—---

If you ask anything of the Father in my name, He will give it to you.

John 16:23

Reflection: At the pinnacle of faith is the belief that Jesus suffered and was crucified so that we may be saved. What's in a name? Not much, unless the name is Jesus, the Christ of God. You can prove to yourself that there is divine power in Jesus' name by following his teachings. We have His word that whatever we ask for in His name shall be granted. This of course implies that we are asking for good things. Today, ask the Lord for the things that are dear to your heart.

Prayer: Jesus, remember me when You come into Your kingdom. In your name, Jesus, I pray for an unending desire to do the will of God.

September 18

Why do you seek the speck in your neighbor's eye but do not notice the log in your own eye?

Matthew 7:3

Reflection: It is easy to criticize others while ignoring our own issues. A friend in an adulterous situation does not need us telling him that adultery is a bad thing. Adults know what is good or bad and know when they have sinned. And so we rarely have to tell anyone that they've done wrong. A better way to bring about a change of heart in other people is to emulate Jesus and show unconditional love and to lead by example. We should never do things that are calculated to make us appear better than another person. Showing unconditional love however does not mean that we are to participate in sinful activities. A wise person knows to avoid places devoted to immorality.

Prayer: Lord, help me to feel secure enough that I will have no urge to judge another person. Holy Spirit, protect me so that as I minster to my friends, I do not become pulled into their sin.

September 19

And hope does not disappoint us because God has poured out His love into our hearts by the Holy Spirit who He has given us.

Romans 5:5

Reflection: Hope in God does not mean that we sit idle. But hope takes away our worries and encourages us to seek after the goodness of the Lord. As difficult as life can be at times, most people admit that they would relive the past so long as they learn valuable lessons. Troubles bring us knowledge and wisdom and can make us better people. Our hope for a better life helps us to seek God. And in turn the love that we experience from God causes our heart and soul to yearn for the purity that only God can bring about.

Prayer: Thank you, Father, for the hope you instilled in me and for Your love which nourishes my soul daily. You have never disappointed me and may I too never disappoint You, or disappoint those around me.

September 20

Forgive us our trespasses as we forgive those who trespass against us...

Matthew 6:12

Reflection: Learning to forgive others is crucial to our happiness and peace of mind. Psychologists have found that people who forgive are happier than people who hang on to grudges. God forgives our bad deeds and so we too must learn how to forgive others and to forgive ourselves. Some people actually make a list of people they would like to forgive and they pray for them. But perhaps the hardest thing is forgiving oneself. The good news is that the harder it is to forgive yourself, the clearer is the indication of remorse, which is what matters to God. If Jesus can forgive the murderer beside Him on the cross, then there is hope of forgiveness for all of us.

Prayer: Spirit of God, please teach me how to forgive others and soften my heart so that I may be cleansed of hate and resentment. Today I will call to mind people that I have not forgiven, so that I might pray for them and pray for myself.

Get wisdom; get insight; do not forget, and do not turn away from the words of My mouth. Do not forsake her, and she will keep you; love her, and she will guard you. The beginning of wisdom is this: Get wisdom, and whatever you get, get insight. Prize her highly, and she will exalt you; she will honor you if you embrace her. She will place on your head a graceful garland; she will bestow on you a beautiful crown.

Proverbs 4:5

Reflection: The world has a lot of highly educated people, but knowledge by itself has not made the most significant difference in our world. Knowledge has brought us terrible weapons and the ability to exploit each other. Conflicts around the world remain the top source of human death and misery. Knowledge is what causes people to develop deadly weapons, while wisdom is what makes others strive for a world without these weapons. Just because we have learned the movement of the stars doesn't mean we have wisdom. The fruit of love is wisdom and this comes from the teachings of the Holy Spirit. It is wisdom that shows us why humility, patience, devotion, repentance, and kindness bring us closer to God. We acquire wisdom by striving for godliness.

Prayer: Lord, teach my heart to understand spiritual truths so that I may be wise. May I value wisdom that comes from You, above knowledge. Today I will search for wisdom in all that comes my way.

September 22

The kingdom of heaven is like a treasure hidden in a field, which someone found and hid; then in his joy, he goes and sells all that he has and buys that field.

Matthew 13:44

Reflection: We like to think of the kingdom of heaven as something up in the sky. But Jesus suggests that even here on earth we can find the kingdom of heaven. The purpose of religion is to show us how we can enjoy life and enjoy it more fully. A life that is devoid of self-examination is a pain riddled life. But when we seek God and find Him and when we make the effort to become devoted to Jesus's teachings, life becomes more peaceful and joyful. But unlike a treasured possession which cannot be duplicated and which can only be owned by a few people at a time, the kingdom of God is unlimited and God's wish is that we will all belong to it. The key to the kingdom comes with an awareness that God has a purpose in mind when He created life, and that purpose is realized in each of us when through our free will, we submit to the Holy Spirit.

Prayer: Father, I have tasted Your love and I know that I should yield completely to the Holy Spirit. Help me to discipline my life so that every day I spend time talking to You and so that I am always willing to give up myself for Your Kingdom.

September 23

---◦◦◦---

They will be divided: father against son and son against father, mother against daughter.

Luke 12:53

Reflection: Jesus tells us in this passage that we may have to make a choice between traditions passed on by our parents, which may not have much to do with God, and his teachings. Faith is not something we inherit from our ancestors. Faith is the result of a choice we make as mature adults to live a spiritual life, to seek God, with full knowledge of what this means. Through our own free will, we must decide if we care about growing the spirit of God that is inside each of us or whether we are more concerned with the tradition we are born into. If our faith in Jesus conflicts with tradition, we are invited to put God above all else.

Prayer: Holy Spirit, whenever there is a conflict between what Jesus teaches and the traditional beliefs of my ancestors, may I have the strength to follow my conscience.

September 24

---∘∘---

How long will you lie there, O lazy bones? When will you rise from your sleep?

Proverbs 6:9

Reflection: Time is precious. When we have zero time left on earth, we die. A day is the same for everyone – twenty-four hours. But some people manage to do a lot of good in these hours while others waste it. The difference between happiness and success often depends on how we spend the time God has given us. When we are using time well, we seem to have a lot of it. But when we are wasting time, it all seems to go away quickly. As well when we waste time we feel guilty. There is so much good we can do when we apply ourselves. Busy people are happy people.

Prayer: Lord, I am sorry for the time I have wasted. Teach me not to be lazy and to appreciate the precious time You have given me on earth. Today I will do my best not to waste time.

Luke the beloved physician greets you, as does Demas.
Colossians 4:14

Reflection: Luke is credited with writing one of the four Gospels and the book of Acts. He was one of the four evangelists, and a martyred Saint. But along with his spiritual devotion, Luke was also a physician, who applied what was known about the physical world to heal people. God can heal the sick and feed the hungry. But part of the divine plan for our world is for the earth to be challenged in many ways. Science has been a very effective tool for learning about our world and there should be no conflict whatsoever between science and spirituality. And so physicians who have learned about the physical body are able to assist the sick. But science can only tell us so much. It cannot tell us about the mind of God. What it can tell us, to the extent that God allows, is how our physical body works. If we take the position that we will accept healing only when it comes through prayer, then we ignore the fact that God created the physical world and has enabled people to understand it for the sake of improving the quality of life.

Prayer: Thank You, Father, for giving us the knowledge to heal and thank You for the physicians who are devoted to healing, and thank You for those physicians who honor their oath to do no harm.

September 26

Take care! Be on your guard against all kinds of greed.
Luke 12:15

Reflection: Our economic system rewards hard work and creativity. The result is that many of us have much more than we could use. And yet some of the happiest moments in life occurs when we were young and naïve and had little money and belongings. For a young person, a run in the park, fresh air and sunshine, was so much fun. Camping out, playing catch, and even reading a book are all free or cheap enjoyable activities. The point is that our happiness does not depend on how much money we have. And, unless we are open to using money to benefit others when required, money brings lots of headaches. If making money becomes its own end, then we are in trouble. We must guard against intense and selfish desire for things which will ultimately be hoarded.

Prayer: Spirit of God, help me to always be a child at heart so that I may continue to enjoy the free things in life that I take for granted. Today I will be receptive to people who need my help.

September 27

---

*Then He said to Thomas, "Put your finger here and see
My hands; and put your hand, and place it in My side.
Do not disbelieve but believe."*

John 20:27

Reflection: Our faith is never perfect. Thomas, an Apostle of Jesus
was present as the Lord healed lepers and yet he still doubted the
divinity of Jesus. So we too can be excused for our doubts. No matter
who we are there is always room to grow in faith. Sometimes we have
no faith and we may even begin to doubt the existence of God or the
divinity of Jesus. And some of us have friends with different views
about life or even different faiths. People we look up to may be atheists
and scoff at our faith. The point is that there are many things in life
which cause us to question our faith. God understands our situation
and so long as we don't suddenly embrace evil, doubts can make our
faith strong. Faith comes by doing those things written in our hearts.

Prayer: God, please help me to understand the things that make me
doubt. Replace my doubts with strong faith. Today I will endeavor to
follow in the steps of Jesus.

September 28

The Lord is my helper; I will not be afraid. What can anyone do to me?

Hebrews 13:6

Reflection: This is a verse that we need to read over and over. These words are meant to remind us that God has dominion over those we are afraid of and those who lord over us. The boss at work, the richest guy in town, the leader of the community – all are subject to God. So we never need to worry about injustice so long as we act in good faith. As such, rather than fear anyone, we should remain devoted to the ways of the Lord. This is our true guarantee for safe passage wherever we are. Furthermore, if we reflect love and forgiveness, we are likely to win our enemies over.

Prayer: Father, help me to love those who persecute me so that my enemies may become my friends. Today I will respect all people but I will fear no one.

September 20

If any of you put a stumbling block before one of these
little ones who believe in Me, it would be better for you
if a great millstone were fastened around your neck and
you were drowned in the depth of the sea.

Matthew 18:6

Reflection: Jesus is talking about children in this passage. In many respects, children are more clear-headed than adults and so the simple message of God is accepted by children, the way it really is. Often standing in the way of fully understanding God's message are the traditions and rituals passed on by parents which take attention away from important things. Sometimes parents are more interested in continuing a cultural tradition than in letting their children follow their conscience. One of the hallmarks of Christianity is that Jesus told his disciples that they were not allowed to coerce anyone into following his teachings. Jesus in this verse is reminding us that it is unwise to coerce others, particularly children, into a belief system that is contrary to their free choice. To respect God is to respect the conscience of other people.

Prayer: God, may I not follow blindly the practices of my ancestors. Give me the strength to be receptive to the direction of the Holy Spirit so that I may put You before any tradition.

September 30

---◦◦---

Such a large crowd of witnesses is all around us! So we must get rid of everything that slows us down, especially the sin that just won't let go. And we must be determined to run the race that is ahead of us.

Hebrews 12:1

Reflection: It is amazing how much we can accomplish when we focus all our energy on a project! This was how countries were able to land people on the moon and to map the entire human genome. With the help of the Holy Spirit we can tackle sins that slow us down. Sin is wickedness, big and small. All sin, sooner or later creates headaches, small and large. Headaches caused by sin make it difficult to move forward. In fact, most of the time, we are busy cleaning up the mess that sins created in our lives. Imagine the energy, time, and resources required to attend to an illicit relationship. Then imagine how much good could have been done with this energy.

Prayer: Holy Spirit, please keep me on the straight and narrow path so that I will not continue to waste the energy that God has given me on selfish and destructive behaviors. Today I will ask Jesus to take away the things that weigh me down as I run the race ahead of me.

October 1

I trusted in your steadfast love; my heart shall rejoice in your salvation.

Psalm 13:5

Reflection: Anyone who trusts in God's love, will rejoice continuously. God delights in our trust and hope in Him. Trusting in God helps us to avoid the snares of the evil one, and to allay our daily fears. Trust in God helps us not to become distracted, thus allowing us to focus our attention on the task at hand. To trust in God is to not let our attention be diverted by doubt and fear. Trust allows us to put in our best effort in the task before us. Where there is trust, there are no worries.

Prayer: Father God, whenever I have doubt or fear, I will pray and trust in You. Today I acknowledge that I have never regretted placing my trust in You.

October 2

When Jesus heard this, he said, "His sickness won't end in death. It will bring glory to God and his Son."

John 11:4

Reflection: Jesus was a man with the Spirit of God in Him. And because Jesus was obedient He was able to do many things which defied physical laws. The spirit within us is capable of the same miracles. Jesus demonstrated this many times. One of His disciples even walked on water. This feat seems supernatural because of the limitations of our physical body. But the spirit within us is not bound by the laws of physics. The most wonderful thing for us is that the Holy Spirit is with us at all times. And for the Spirit of God, nothing is impossible. We are invited to take advantage of God's love. Jesus brought a dead man to life partly to demonstrate that we too can do even more.

Prayer: Lord, thank You for keeping my fears at bay and for blessing me beyond my imagination. Spirit of God, help me to realize the power of God within me. Today I will focus on living in the spirit.

October 3

Consider how far you have fallen! Repent and do the things you did at first. If you do not repent, I will come to you and remove your lampstand from its place.

Revelation 2:5

Reflection: How much will a parent rejoice over one child that manages to turn his life around after a life of wild living? The overwhelming majority of people eventually come to reject wild life because guilt does turn people around. Researchers from the University of Waterloo, Canada, found that when people feel guilt, they actually feel heavier! Guilt-ridden people estimate their body weight as heavier than it actually is. Guilt literally weighs people down. Not surprisingly, it has become very clear that guilt is built into us to check our behavior. It is precisely because we have a conscience that we can be held responsible for the choices we make. Every day God calls us to repentance and to accept His Grace.

Prayer: Thank You, God, for giving me guilt as a guide for my behavior. Today and every day, I pray that there will be rejoicing in heaven, because of my choices on earth.

October 4

I am the way, and the truth, and the life. No one comes to the Father except through Me.

John 14:6

Reflection: Does this mean that non-Christians are doomed? One way to understand this passage is to ask what it is that Jesus stands for. Jesus is about repentance, forgiveness and redemption. Anyone who has ever been guilty of wickedness is in need of repentance and redemption. Everyone who practices love and forgiveness is following the teachings of Jesus and could not be truly hostile to Jesus. In all faiths, there are people who love God and there is no doubt that the Holy Spirit guides people to the truth and the path of love. Indeed Jesus healed people from various faiths. A claim that there is no salvation outside of Jesus might sound to some, like nonsense, and divisive. But there is no salvation until we are prepared to renounce wickedness in all its form and to accept God's teachings, to love one another and to love God. Everyone who resolves to do the will of God will not shun the teachings of Jesus because there is no greater spiritual truth. If the world practiced this teaching, wars and violence would come to an end.

Prayer: Father, I pray that I will love all people regardless of their faith, and that I will never forget that Jesus died for me when I didn't yet know Him. I pray that my actions today will reflect the love that Jesus teaches.

October 3

------◦◦------

For God so loved the world that He gave His only Son, so that who believes in Him may not perish but may have eternal life.

John 3:16

Reflection: The suffering Son of God. This is an amazing story and until a person experiences firsthand the gifts of the Holy Spirit, the Gospel seems like nonsense. The idea that God would have a Son then stand by while His Son is innocently crucified with thieves is highly improbable. Yet this is the belief of billions of Christians. And anyone who has attempted to walk the straight and narrow road, will testify to the power and wisdom of the Gospel. We cannot explain everything about God because God does not consult with us. Nonetheless, life provides us with sufficient opportunities to experience the difference between a contrite and obedient lifestyle, and an undisciplined carefree life. Next time someone tells you that there is no God, invite him to become devoted to a life of love, learning, and wisdom. Invite him to practice the teachings of Jesus for twenty-four hours. People walking towards God, usually encounter Jesus along the way.

Prayer: Thank You, Father, for the gift of Your Son and for the gift of the Holy Spirit. Thank You Jesus for carrying my sins on Your shoulders. May I always be cheerful as I carry my cross.

October 6

By this all people will know that you are My disciples, if you have love for one another.

John 13:35

Reflection: A priest who had been raised as a non-Christian once revealed why he converted from his native Eastern religion to Christianity. In his native culture one shunned an enemy. Then, one day, he learned that Jesus taught that we are to love and to pray for our enemies. He was so impressed by the wisdom in this teaching that he inquired further about Jesus. Eventually, the Holy Spirit led him to the priesthood. This priest's conversion demonstrates that the laws of God are written in his heart and so he was able to recognize the truth about Jesus. Because we all have good in us we are able to recognize the goodness of the Lord.

Prayer: Spirit of God, open my heart so that I do not stubbornly hold on to beliefs or traditions which are not of You. Today, teach me to love those who persecute me.

October 7

The one who is righteous will live by faith.

Romans 1:17

Reflection: To be righteous is to forego many harmful pleasures in the hope that life will offer more satisfying opportunities. Our faith is that when we live a disciplined life we will emerge happier than those who don't discipline their behavior. "Faith" is often a misunderstood concept. Faith never requires us to do something that is contrary to love or to common sense. And faith does not ask us to sit back and expect manna to fall from heaven. But as we struggle to be obedient to the prodding of the Spirit within us, faith asks that we not give up when the going gets tough. Faith makes us relax after we have done all that we can, and to trust in God that all will be well. Faith asks us to seek life in the spirit, rather than life in the flesh. Jesus asks us to live a moral life.

Prayer: Spirit of God, strengthen my faith as I struggle to carry my cross of faith behind Jesus.

October 8

It is for freedom that Christ set us free; therefore keep standing firm and do not be subject again to a yoke of slavery.

Galatians 5:1

Reflection: Faith in God means that we do not need to worship idols or to be held captive to sinful habits. In many countries, laws which regulate morality are being removed, thereby allowing activities such as gambling, marijuana, prostitution, adultery, and Sunday shopping. Some people see this as a bad thing; and undoubtedly, many of these activities are undesirable, and even sinful. But, laws do not make people moral. God has made us free to live as we please but this, of course, comes with consequences. And there is no doubt that this trend towards greater social freedom in countries around the world, will continue. God wants us to freely choose how we live and not be forced to behave one way or another by human laws which do not change hearts. Freedom in Christ means that we have freely chosen to abide by his teachings, and have thus been freed from the captivity of sin.

Prayer: Thank You, Father, for my freedom. Help me to use this freedom to promote love and understanding amongst the people in my life. Today I will live as a person freed from the chains of sins.

October 9

If any of you lacks wisdom, let him ask God who gives generously to all without reproach, and it will be given him.

James 1:5-8

Reflection: Until our heart is pure we are still lacking in wisdom. And so it is always a good idea for us to take time and to reflect before we do things. Christianity is love in action. Yet God loves even those who do not know Jesus. Religion is not a competition amongst people. There is only one God, and God is love. We must each find the courage to question what we are taught and what we believe. The point of spirituality is to guide us so that we can learn love and compassion. And we have to find the courage to let others, especially our family members, search for God freely.

Prayer: Father, give me the wisdom and strength to reject teachings or traditions which may have been passed down to me, which do not promote love and forgiveness.

October 10

There is neither Jew nor Greek, there is neither slave nor free, there is no male and female, for you are all one in Christ Jesus.

Galatians 3:28

Reflection: Jesus had Jewish lineage but He interacted with Jews and non-Jews alike. He healed many people who were not Jewish. Through Jesus salvation came to all people. There is only one God and His desire is the salvation of all people. A lot of the turmoil in the world today arises from the failure of people to acknowledge the common origin and common destiny of all people. This failure is at the root of sectarian wars and the reason that we put so many resources into making guns and weapons. Each side in war, is told that the people on the other side are different from them and wish to hurt them. The worst of it, is when people use God to justify hate and violence. Apostle Paul emphasizes in the letter written to believers in Galatia, that there is only one brand of Christianity, and that neither ethnicity nor nationality has a bearing on their salvation.

Prayer: Father, help me to nourish the fact that this is Your world and that other humans are Your children and therefore, my brothers and sisters. Today I will pray for peace on earth.

October 11

Exercise is good for your body, but religion helps you in every way. It promises life now and forever.

1 Timothy 4:8-9

Reflection: There are many benefits of regular physical exercise to the body. To exercise the soul, we need religion. Today skeptics point to religious people who are violent and revengeful as evidence that religion is not a good thing. But these skeptics confuse the religious with those who use religion to justify hate and wickedness. These type of people are found in every religion. Jesus was very clear, that whatever we do to each other must be grounded in love. It is through practicing love that we open up the life that Jesus talked about. Religion is about love and wisdom. There is no doubt that if people practice the teachings of Jesus, the world would be a much better and happier place.

Prayer: Father, help me always to follow the peaceful and loving path set out by Jesus so that my religious practice will always be a blessing to others.

October 12

Do not be anxious about anything but in everything,
by prayer and petition, with thanksgiving, present your
requests to God.

Philippians 4:6

Reflection: After waiting for weeks to hear from the doctor's office, Linda learned that she was healthy, she was not dying. This good news immediately made life so much richer and more fun for her. At that point she realized that she had taken a lot for granted and had never appreciated how good she had it. That afternoon Linda went for a long walk, she soaked in the fresh air and the rays of the sun never felt better on her face. We have a lot to be grateful to God for. Learning to give thanks and to count our blessings bring humility and joy. One of the biggest gifts we have is each other. We should make more effort to show those around us how much we appreciate them and to thank God for all the wonderful people that cross our paths daily.

Prayer: Father God, thank You for my family, thank You for my friends, thank You for my teachers and for my co-workers.

October 13

So do not worry about tomorrow, for tomorrow will bring worries of its own; today's trouble is enough for today.

Matthew 6:34

Reflection: We all have a habit of self-torture by speculation on all the negative things that could happen to us. This verse is another great example of how practical the teachings of our Savior are. Jesus is not asking us to live as if there will be no tomorrow! Just that after we have done all that is within our power, we are best to trust God. We need to accept that we do not have control over every aspect of life. This, however, is easier said than done especially if we have an anxious personality. Nevertheless, the things we fear never happen and God never allows us to experience things which will overwhelm us. Jesus invites us to put our trust in the Father rather than to stress over the unknown.

Prayer: Father God, only You know tomorrow and only You know what lies ahead for me. I pray that I will always trust in Your loving grace.

October 14

Ask and it will be given you; search and you will find;
knock and the door will be opened for you.

Matthew 7:7

Reflection: Sometimes we feel that we are bothering God, that it is unfair to keep calling on God for every little thing. The fact is that God wants us to keep calling on Him, for everything, as often as we need to. Jesus is encouraging us in this passage to form a habit of calling on God with our questions or requests. We are curious creatures and so we are always searching. There is nothing wrong with this. But when we call on God, we have to learn to listen patiently as God reveals to us the answers to our questions.

Prayer: Lord, I know that You answer my questions often by changing my perspective, so that I may understand some of the mysteries of life. Please help me to be patient as You teach me about myself and about the world around me.

October 15

I will give to the Lord the thanks due to his righteousness,
and sing praise to the name of the Lord, the most high.
Psalm 7:17

Reflection: As Jesus demonstrated, God is not interested in the types of accolades we give to kings and queens. This is one of the reasons why many of us do not appreciate the extent to which God sustains us on a daily basis. God has demonstrated His love for us in countless ways and by giving up His Son at the prime of his life to suffering and humiliation, all for our sake. Despite all the misfortunes around us we know that God has not cursed but blessed us more than we deserve. How much thanks can we give to God who keeps us safe and who adopts us as children despite our constant disobedience? When we are sent by God to minister to a destitute alcoholic, and find out that the person has been praying for help from God, we can't help but be teary-eyed that God has not given up on him. We may not be alcoholic and we may not have drug issues, but in our own ways, we are just as destitute as any addict is. God loves the poorest and the disobedient as much as He loves the most obedient. This is our God.

Prayer: Father, I cannot thank You enough for all that You do for me and for my brothers and sisters. May the way that I treat other people demonstrate my gratitude for Your saving Grace.

October 16

Even though I walk through the darkest valley, I fear no evil.

Psalm 23:4

Reflection: The darkest valley is not the type of place we wish to be, because we are vulnerable to attacks from the top of the mountain. But life often takes us through scary places like this. In times of trouble we imagine the worst outcome and we tremble with fear. This is when faith should come to our aid and relieve us of worry and stress. If we believe in God, how could we ever be fearful of anything? Fear from this point of view is a sin and a manifestation of lack of trust in God. And we are all guilty of this. As we draw closer, we learn that love drives out fear and that too much love of self can create fear. Jesus went ahead of us into the darkest valley.

Prayer: Lord, I know that Your rod and Your staff comfort me as I walk through the valley of death. Help me to trust You in all aspects of my life so that I will remain steadfast even when I cannot see the road ahead.

October 17

All things are lawful for me, but not all things are helpful.
All things are lawful for me, but I will not be enslaved
by anything.

1 Corinthians 6:12

Reflection: Slavery is not just about whips and chains. Having a bad habit can be a worse form of slavery. Alcoholism and other addictions are terrible diseases that tend to run in families. We all know good talented people who have been destroyed by addictions. Sometimes people resort to drinking too much, as a result of loneliness, laziness, or self-esteem issues. People also drink to forget. But there is a good alternative to addiction. It is spirituality. Life in the spirit is very invigorating. A person who starts the day in prayer is less likely to be controlled by addiction. And so we see that aside from teaching us how to love and to be charitable, God will remove the yoke of sin from us, if we let Him.

Prayer: Father, I pray for people with addictions. I pray that these people will turn their hearts to You and learn to feel love again and I pray that the Holy Spirit will help me to recognize the bad habits in my life. Today I will not be enslaved by sin.

October 18

And so, for sure, will wisdom be to your soul: find it
and you will have a future and your hope will not be
cut short.

Proverbs 24:14

Reflection: Wisdom is at the top of the list of God's gifts to us, and
where there is wisdom there is hope, and where there is peace there
is opportunity for growth. Research from the University of Toronto
shows that people who feel less hopeful for the present and the future
are at a greater risk of becoming involved in destructive behaviors,
such as using drugs or committing crimes. Hope grows when we are
willing to confront who we are, and are willing to allow the Holy Spirit
to mold us. If we put in effort to pray, read scripture and meditate
regularly, we will not be without hope or wisdom.

Prayer: I pray for people in jails and for the sick. May You use me,
Father, to bring hope and understanding to some of these people.
Today I will renew my hope in Jesus.

October 19

Greater love has no one than this, that He lay down His life for His friends.

John 15:13

Reflection: Every so often we read about heroes who risked their lives to save others. Many of these heroes often survive, thanks be to God. Jesus on the other hand knew that He would die when he laid His life down for everyone. He did so out of love and compassion. Jesus's sacrifice is not comparable to people who kill themselves along with innocent people because they have hate. People who kill because of hate derive satisfaction from the fact they have struck their enemies. Jesus on the other, hand felt so much compassion for people that He was willing to take on death so that humanity might have hope. Jesus could have done away with His enemies, but as part of the Divine plan of redemption, Jesus was obedient to God's will. This alone should bring joy to our hearts all day long.

Prayer: Spirit of God, help me to be there for my friends and families. I pray for people who are so angry and hateful that they are willing to kill people. I pray that they will hear your voice and soften their hearts.

October 20

We are always confident; even though we know that while we are at home in the body, we are always away from the Lord for we walk by faith.

2 Corinthians 5:6

Reflection: The human spirit and consciousness are clothed in a physical body. A body is a physical trait that we share with lower animals. Even then we have the most beautiful body in the animal kingdom. Only human beings stand upright. Our appearance is refined and elegant. Nonetheless our ancestors became a part of the physical world because they were disobedient. It was only after Adam sinned that he realized that he was naked. So this physical body that we have is a limitation, which separates us from God, for God is Spirit. When we rejected to live as children in paradise and chose to know evil, our body took its present form according to the calculus of God, to exist alongside our original spirit. Jesus came and took the human form to guide us back to the state that God prepared for us.

Prayer: In You, Jesus, I place my trust. Help me to fully enjoy and appreciate my life here on earth, as I look forward to an even greater existence.

October 21

Humility is the fear of the Lord; its wages are riches and honor and life.

Proverbs 22:4

Reflection: Humility is probably the highest of virtues. It is humility that melts away anger. It is humility that enables one to repent and to make amends. Greatness is expressed by humility and wisdom. Let the great person bear the burden of others and let her lead by example of love and forgiveness. The greatness that God recognizes in us involves the ability to hold one's tongue in check at all times and the ability to refrain from damaging the character of other people. Great people make those around them feel great.

Prayer: Father, You delight in the humble and contrite heart. Help me to treat others with respect and love so that I never come across as condescending.

October 22

The wise have eyes in their head, but fools walk in darkness.

Ecclesiastes 2:14

Reflection: This verse reminds us that what we perceive with our senses, depends on where we are spiritually. It is important to seek wisdom which comes from heeding the teachings of our Christ. Wisdom is what enables us to appreciate the information we receive and to use it for the common good. Free will is about choices. However, every choice has consequences. But often, we do not see these consequences at the time of behavior. This is why it is a good thing to develop a regular prayer life which will help us to gain in wisdom and to develop healthy habits. The more reflective we are, the easier it is to anticipate outcomes. Plus, the teachings of Jesus will help us avoid pitfalls. The details that a wise person takes away from a scene, eludes a naïve or foolish person.

Prayer: Holy Spirit, open my heart so that my senses might see more. Help me to deal with the sins which cause me to misunderstand Your teachings.

October 23

For we all stumble in many ways. If someone does not
stumble in what he says, he is a perfect individual, able
to control the entire body as well.

James 3:2

Reflection: The first step in changing for the better is to realize that
we have faults. The next step is to understand the nature of these faults.
It is after we know our weaknesses that we can begin to appreciate
the help of the Holy Spirit. Many of those who rejected Jesus saw
themselves as perfect and so one of the charges against Jesus, was
that He was often in the company of "terrible" sinners. Unlike the
Pharisees who were "high and mighty", and never saw themselves in
need of assistance, Jesus was comfortable among sinners, and happy in
the company of those who appreciated His attention. All have sinned,
but some have difficulty facing up to this truth. So let us remember
that what we think, what we say, what we do or do not do, can be
sinful. Our entire body must be under control, not just our outward
behavior.

Prayer: Jesus, my heart agrees with Your teachings and I know that I
fall short many times. Thank You for the gift of the Holy Spirit

October 24

―――――○○――――

Remember those who are in prison, as though in prison
with them, and those who are mistreated, since you are
also in the body.

Hebrews 13:3

Reflection: It is usually not the rich and powerful people that need our attention or that need assistance from governments. People who are marginalized should be at the top of our priorities for assistance. We often think of offenders in prisons as people who deserve what they got because they had made bad choices. Many of them have. But studies show that serious mental illness, such as schizophrenia, is eight times more prevalent in people who are in prison than in the general population. Fifty percent of women in jail suffer from clinical depression. Many offenders come from very troubled backgrounds and are the product of foster homes. And so it is, that offenders themselves are often victims. Reaching out to people in trouble can be very fulfilling. Paul's letter above was written for the benefit of people who were being mistreated on account of their faith, nonetheless, it is our Christian duty to remember people who are sick or in trouble.

Prayer: Father, I thank You that You never forget anyone. I pray for people who reach out to all needy people regardless of what they have done. May Your Spirit guide and protect them. Today I will pray for everyone that is experiencing a crisis in their lives.

October 25

Only Jesus has the power to save! His name is the only one in all the world that can save anyone.

Acts 4:12

Reflection: We all accept that we have been guilty of wickedness at one time or another. While we did not ask to be born into the world, we have a responsibility to treat other people fairly because we have free will. When we fail to behave properly we deserve to be sanctioned. This is similar to a parent disciplining a child. Jesus, through complete obedience to the will of God and through his experience on earth, has the power to cancel our sins. The prodigal son left his parents because he thought he could do better, but his parents never stopped loving him. This is our faith, but how God saves people, or who God will save, is in a sense not our business. Our business is to reflect the love of God to each other and to be prepared with answers for those who question our faith. We spread the word of God not by judging other people, but by letting people see how we are blessed by the Lord and how the teachings of Jesus have transformed us. Salvation came from Jesus.

Prayer: Spirit of God, may I always remember that You loved me when I was yet a sinner and that I am in no position to pass judgment on to my brother. Today I acknowledge Jesus as my Lord and Savior.

October 26

Do not judge so that you may not be judged. For with the judgment you make, you will be judged and the measure you give will be the measure you get.

Matthew 7:1

Reflection: There are several reasons why Jesus tells us not judge others. For one thing, we will never have sufficient information about each other to enable us to reach a fair assessment. Another reason is that when it comes to moral issues, we are answerable to God, the Giver of life and not to each other. In fact, one of the effects of judging others is that we become complacent and ignore our own misdeeds. Again Jesus, out of love for us, reminds us to be careful, that we do not hold each other to a standard that we ourselves fall short of.

Prayer: Lord, help me not judge so that I may not be judged. Thank You for forgetting my sins.

October 27

For the Lord hears the needy and does not despise His own people who are prisoners.

Psalm 69:33

Reflection: In many cases people become needy or are in prisons as a result of bad choices. This verse tells us that such people are dear to God. Many of the difficulties we run into as humans are self-induced and this is one reason why we as Christians have a duty to live by example. The Holy Spirit works through us to reach other people. A study from America found that inmates who attend ten or more Bible studies in a one-year period prior to being released were less likely to return to jail. But we don't need to be locked up to experience prison. People who have no regard for the happiness of others are imprisoned by their conscience. Regular prayer and Bible studies liberate us from the snare of the devil and gives us more freedom to live life more fully. Let us remember people around the world, who are imprisoned and even killed because of their faith in Jesus.

Prayer: Father, I know that there are people in many parts of the world who are not free to worship according to their conscience. Today I pray that the Holy Spirit will bless and minister to these people.

October 28

Go therefore and make disciples of all nations, baptizing
them in the name of the Father and of the Son and of the
Holy Spirit,

Matthew 28:19

Reflection: Christianity is not a tribal religion although the faith
originated from Judaism and was spread primarily by the Romans.
Every human being is dear to God. As countries around the world
become more multi-cultural it is becoming fashionable to embrace
faith practices from non-Christian places. Young people especially,
are not wanting to learn about Jesus, because they see Christianity
as a dominant religion and the faith practiced by many people whom
they disagree with. Yet the most desirable countries in the world today
are where the teachings of Jesus are practiced daily – love, tolerance,
charity, freedom of religion, and equality. Young people may wish
to remain open, and even to explore other faith practices, but in the
end each person is invited by God to follow teachings which promote
love and tolerance and which are not based on tribalism. There is only
one God.

Prayer: Spirit of God, the more I learn about Jesus the more I aspire
to become his servant. Help me to remain faithful to Jesus' values of
love, peace and charity. Today I pray that everyone who sees me will
be reminded of Jesus.

October 29

Go into all the world and preach the gospel to all creation.

Mark 16:15

Reflection: Jesus said this to his disciples and to all those who chose to follow him. The internet, social media, and air travel are some of the things that have brought the world closer. Young people around the world want the type of freedom enjoyed in the West. Let us never forget that Europe and North America became promised lands for most of the world's migrants only after the basic tenets of Christianity–love, equality of all people, freedom to vote, freedom of religion, and the rule of law for all citizens, became the foundation in these societies. There are many ways to preach the Gospel. Many Christians did so by ending the slave trade, and providing free hospitals and houses of refuge around the world. Christianity civilized the modern world, and Christians are at the forefront of the largest charities in the world.

Prayer: Father, the world would be a better place if there was more love and forgiveness. Today I will try to reflect the teachings of Jesus to those I come across.

October 30

And may they come to their senses and escape from the
snare of the devil, after being captured by him to do his
will.

2 Timothy 2:26

Reflection: To be snared by the devil is to be tricked. We get trapped
by evil because evil stimulates the pleasure area of the brain. Evil can
be pleasurable, even if the pleasure doesn't last. Evil often stems from
hate or selfishness, and we all read about people who have become
slaves to hate, and think it is okay to kill people. To escape a snare is
to become free. But freedom comes with responsibilities. When we
abuse our free will, through bad health choices or bad moral choices,
we stand in danger of having our freedom taken from us. People who
smoke may develop lung problems which prevent them from living
well. Everything we do has consequences. Lifestyle choices with no
regard for others may bring short-term pleasure but it also brings
slavery and long-lasting troubles. And so we see that evil is like a net
which a fisherman uses to snare unsuspecting fish.

Prayer: Father, thank You for blessing me with so much freedom.
Help me to show my appreciation by making wise choices. Today I
will flee from evil.

October 31

*For God did not send His Son to the world to condemn
the world but to save the world through Him.*

John 3:17

Reflection: Jesus came to herald the period of grace. Jesus showed through his life and through the miracles he performed, that the way of the world leads to destruction. The Bible tells us that there is no one who is good, no one who does the Will of God at all times. Anything short of the Will of God is not only disobedience but wickedness; and wickedness, as we know, is at the root of human misery. Yet, what we experience from God despite our disobedience is love and a chance at redemption. Jesus did not come to condemn but to redeem us. Jesus did not come to punish us for sin but to help us see the error of our choices. It is for our own good that God is interested in the choices we make. Jesus's life says to us: "Follow me to the Father." On this last day of October, we should ignore the world around us celebrating things of the devil, but think only of God.

Prayer: Spirit of God, help our leaders to promote laws which encourage people to choose love over hate and compassion over greed. Today I will be mindful of the things in my life that offend my conscience, and offend the teachings of Jesus, and refrain from all practices that dishonor God.

November 1 — All Saints Day

I say to the Lord, "You are my master; I have nothing good apart from you."

Psalm 16:2

Reflection: People often say that we don't need God to be good. Yet no one aside of Jesus has ever shown us how to be good. This is not meant as a disrespect for other historical figures, but the fact is that no one has ever told people to pray for those who persecute them, or to love other people as much as we love ourselves, and then give up His life to demonstrate this teaching. Our world is sinful. Our parents are sinful. We are born into sin. Most of us even break the hearts of our loved ones. We are unfaithful in our relationships. Left alone, without God, we would probably destroy the world with deadly weapons and begin to enslave each other again. It is the Spirit of God which keeps us humble and opened to the will of God. All good within us comes from God.

Prayer: Father God, when I am honest with myself I see that my desires are all about myself and do not always reflect consideration for other people. May I always be humble to say that any good in me comes from my God.

November 2 — All Souls Day

―――⊸∘⊸―――

But the advocate, the Holy Spirit, whom the Father
will send in My name, will teach you all things and will
remind you of everything I have said to you.

John 14:26

Reflection: Some people believe that after God created the world, God stepped back from human affairs. But this idea denies the significance of Jesus and it denies the presence of the Holy Spirit in the world. Christians believe that God is involved actively in human affairs, and that God delivers those who seek Him. Drug and alcohol addictions are two of the most debilitating diseases in our society. Friends and families watch as their loved one is held captive and slowly destroyed by addiction. The addict is often powerless to stop the addiction, his only hope is intervention. But the addict must desire change, otherwise there is no point. The human condition is comparable to that of an addict. Sin is so embedded in our nature that our hope is deliverance by God. For this purpose Jesus came and left us with the Holy Spirit.

Prayer: Father, help me to stop rationalizing wrongdoings. Help me to never forget that I have the gift of the Holy Spirit to help me carry my cross daily behind my Savior. Today I will make more effort to demonstrate the relevance of Jesus in my life.

November 3

On the Sabbath He began to teach in the synagogue,
and many who heard Him were astounded. They said,
"Where did this man get all this?"

Mark 6:2-6

Reflection: Atheists accuse Christians of creating a God in their image. Religious leaders during the time of Jesus had their own idea of how God operates. To their dismay, it was the son of the carpenter and not a person formally trained in scripture that claimed to be the Son of God. Jesus spent a lot of time among outcasts. In the thirty years that Jesus walked the Earth, He probably spent more time in prayer than people who lived one hundred years. He was loving, He was compassionate, and He remained humble throughout. No wonder at His young age, He was so receptive to the Spirit of His Father, that it was a young Jesus who taught the elders around him about wisdom and about love. Jesus demonstrated with His teachings that wisdom is a gift from God and not something we learn from the pages of books, necessarily.

Prayer: Holy Spirit, make my heart gentle so that I may follow Jesus faithfully and so that I may be receptive to Your teachings.

November 4

---—◦—---

*So, because you are lukewarm – neither hot nor cold – I
am about to spit you out of my mouth.*

Revelation 3:16

Reflection: We all know people who agree with everyone, because they
wish to avoid conflicts. It can be a good thing to shun confrontation,
unless in so doing we are misleading people about our faith. People
who go whichever way the wind blows on spiritual matters are the
ones likely to tell you that every religion is the same. They may be
people who see themselves as "good people" and not in need of rebirth
or renewal. They don't see the need for God in human affairs. They
stand for nothing except for what is currently popular. On the other
hand it is easier to have discussions with those who are cold because
they know where they stand and they are willing to defend their
position. Apostle Paul was initially cold on Jesus. He persecuted the
followers of Jesus and he approved of the stoning of Jesus's followers.
But as soon as Paul knew Jesus, he devoted the remainder of his life
to spreading the good news about Jesus. Paul was never lukewarm, he
went from cold to hot.

Prayer: Father, may I always be ready to examine my heart in light of
Your love so that I may remain steadfast in Your teachings, and remain
hot, like the Apostle Paul. Today I will remain hot in my faith.

November 5

Do your best to present yourself to God as one approved, a worker who does not need to be ashamed and who correctly handles the word of truth.

2 Timothy 2:15

Reflection: The requirement for serving God is a contrite heart and desire for a purer heart, something that we are all capable of. Notice that people tend to dress like people in their social or professional circles. The reason for this is that we all feel the need to conform. Cults thrive on this desire to be like each other, by making people follow silly rules they keep their members in tow. Even if we don't belong to cults we may still wish to be like colleagues we respect. If our friends or colleagues do not share our faith, we hide our faith (to "hide one's light under a bushel" as the Scripture says). This is not necessary, people do not react negatively to us because of faith. It is only if our faith does not promote love and tolerance that people react negatively. Hypocrisy is what people reject. And so let us freely live our faith to promote love and understanding among the children of God.

Prayer: Father, help me to shine Your love on people around me so that I may model Jesus's teachings to all I come across. Today I will present myself ready for the directions of the Holy Spirit.

November 6

———◦———

Do not rejoice when your enemy falls. And do not let your heart be glad when he stumbles.

Proverbs 24:17

Reflection: When we envy other people or when we are jealous of their achievements, we tend to delight in their misfortunes. But envy and jealousy also make us depressed. Envy generally arises out of our need to control everything around us and so we feel threatened by people who pose a threat to things we hold dear. In many cases, our fear is not real, just our imagination. One way to deal with envy is to focus on our own gifts and put them to use. It is not Christ like to wish other people bad, or to rejoice in their troubles.

Prayer: Lord, help me to never envy or compare myself to others. Instead, help me to always trust in Your saving grace and fairness.

November 7

You will be punished if you make fun of someone in trouble

Proverb 17:5

Reflection: It is almost inconceivable to imagine a Christian making fun of someone in trouble. Indeed when people are in trouble we have a duty to reach out to them. To do so is not to suggest that the person is blameless. Sometimes our news media flourish on spreading bad news, gossip and the misfortunes of others. We should avoid hearing gossips. Christianity is about working to increase human happiness.

Prayer: Father God, Please help me to appreciate how much You have covered my troubles, and may I console people I meet rather than make fun of them.

November 8

For if you forgive men their trespasses, your heavenly Father will also forgive you.

Luke 23:34

Reflection: Jesus said that we are to forgive our adversaries because it is the best way to win them over. After all God wants to see every one changed for good. Mahatma Gandhi, Martin Luther King, and Nelson Mandela, are three leaders who chose peaceful resistance and a path of forgiveness, rather than violence to confront their opponents. As a result, lives were saved. One of the government ministers responsible for the death of thousands of people in South Africa, would later wash the feet of many of those he wronged. "I have sinned against the Lord and against you! Will you forgive me?" he said to his victims. Today the three leaders are remembered and revered, while violent leaders are despised and soon forgotten. This is an illustration of the wisdom of Jesus in action.

Prayer: Father, may I be remembered as a person of peace and forgiveness. Today I will call to mind some of Your servants who have promoted peace and harmony.

November 9

The stone that the builders rejected has become the
corner stone.

Mark 12:10

Reflection: The religious leaders at the time of Jesus were certain
that they would recognize the Messiah whenever He came. They were
looking out for a Messiah to restore the Kingdom of David, and in so
doing overthrow the Romans. They were so focused on the outward
appearance of meek and humble Jesus, and the fact that he was not
born into a priestly family, that they rejected Jesus as the one that they
had been waiting for. Today, we too make the mistake of attaching too
much importance to the trappings of human power. The fact is that
there are many ordinary folks who do not occupy important positions
but who are out there making a difference in other people's lives.

Prayer: Spirit of God, open my heart so that I may not be misled by
appearance, and in so doing reject those You have sent to help me and
to teach me.

November 10

Give instructions to a wise man and he will be wiser;
teach a righteous man and he will increase learning.

Proverbs 9:9

Reflection: A paraphrase to this might be: a word to the wise is sufficient. A wise man is the man who humbles himself enough to learn from the events of his life. A wise man is the man who refuses to accept the status quo and yearns for a purer heart. A good child is a delight to her parents. Churches, temples, mosques, and synagogues, are everywhere, reminding us that there is a spiritual requirement to a full life. Spirituality is about rising above pettiness, rising above the desires of the flesh. When we grow our spirituality the energy within us will be sustained forever. Our conscience may not rebuke us for not knowing God but it admonishes us when we engage in wickedness. A desire to confront our wickedness opens our heart to God. We should be like Solomon and ask God to give us wisdom.

Prayer: Father, seeking to know you is wisdom. Grant that I may cherish wisdom so that I will watch what I say and have control over my thoughts.

November 11 — Remembrance/Armistice Day, a day to celebrate peace and the end of conflicts

---

For the gate is narrow and the road is hard that leads to life, and there are few who find it.

Matthew 7:14

Reflection: To enter the narrow gate that Jesus speaks of we will need to shed a lot of bad things, including violence and hypocrisy. When we begin to take our spirituality seriously, we quickly realize how much we need to be cleansed and what we need to watch for daily. Old habits are not easy to break, especially when we have come to depend on these habits to cope with life. But if some of our habits are less than good, then we must shed them. In a world with so many temptations, this may be hard, but there is nothing that prayer or devotion cannot solve. The good news is that the straight and narrow road that Jesus speaks of is also the most exciting and fulfilling road. As we shed the heavy load of sin that we carry, we are better able to enjoy life.

Prayer: Spirit of God, help me to never forget that regular prayer and devotion help to keep me closer to You and help me to shed bad habits, as well as live in peace and harmony with my fellow humans.

November 12

Do not judge by appearances but judge with the right judgment.

John 7:24

Reflection: Every so often, we come across people that surprise us because they are so down-to-earth. They don't have fancy titles or accolades and often have no public recognition. One such woman adopted a difficult baby and raised him lovingly while facing all the challenges that come with bringing up a child with fetal alcohol syndrome. This woman never complained, always had a smile, and even now that the boy is in his twenties, her love for him is as strong as ever despite the headaches and difficulties that he causes her. Without such a loving mother, this young man would have likely caused much havoc to society. The Lord sees her work and the Lord rewards her accordingly, but her work will never be known to most of us.

Prayer: Help me, Lord, to remember and to honor in my prayers, those who work selflessly unrecognized; bless their work even when others fail to recognize their contributions.

November 13

---⊸◦⊸---

For the Lord disciplines those whom He loves, and chastises every child whom He accepts.

Hebrew 12:6

Reflection: We may observe with some frustration that drawing closer to God does not entirely relieve us of disappointments or even pain. It may even be that we perceive our correction to be occurring with more frequency as we draw closer to God. However, it is more likely the case that we come to notice our failings more after we resolve to become more spiritual. If the Father who made us did not love us so much, we would be discarded and the energy used to sustain us would be put to other use. But God has yet greater things in store for us, and so the discipline of the Holy Spirit is designed to cleanse us as we join others who labor in the vineyard. The cleaner we are the better we are able to serve other people and the less likely we are to bring shame to God.

Prayer: Thank You Father for being gentle with me as You prepare me for bigger and greater things. Help me to have wise and loving answers for all those who inquire about You.

November 14

The teachings of the wise are a fountain of life that one may turn away from the snares of death.

Proverbs 13:14

Reflection: Next time you receive loving and kind words from a friend or family member, show gratitude. Wisdom is what makes us turn the other cheek and pray for our enemies. When we strive to be faithful to our marriage vow, we bless the children of the marriage. When we seek to pursue goodness and to live with a purer heart, we are choosing the path of wisdom. It is also wise not to run from the Lord even after we have been unfaithful to His teachings. God is full of love and kindness and He never rejects a repentant heart. When the Bible speaks of "death", it is referring to a life without redemption, a life that is permanently separated from God. No one ever regrets abiding in God or regrets seeking out the company of those who seek after God.

Prayer: Lord, let me drink from Your fountain so that I may never be thirsty again. Today I pray that the Holy Spirit will guide me away from the snares of death and all its empty promises.

November 15

Who is going to harm you if you are eager to do good? But
even if you should suffer for what is right, you are blessed.
"Do not fear what they fear; do not be frightened."

1 Peter 3:13-14

Reflection: A lot of fear arises from our hesitancy to accept the idea that God has forgiven us. It makes no sense to believe in a loving all-powerful God while at the same time fearful that we will meet with doom. One of the biggest sources of our joy, even when we are in the midst of pain, should be the assurance that the Father is in control and has plans for our life. But God's plan for us is not just about going to heaven; the earth is full of beauty and adventures and interesting people. If we chase after goodness on earth, we shall find peace, joy, and fulfillment in our daily walk. Our earth was not designed to be a place of suffering. Indeed Jesus came so that we might live life more fully.

Prayer: Father, thank You for giving me life and thank You for Your Son, Jesus, and thank You for the teachings in my heart. Today as I count my blessings, I will enjoy all the beautiful things around me.

November 16

But about that day and hour, no one knows, neither the angels of heaven, not the Son, but only the Father.

Matthew 24:36

Reflection: A wise person treats each day as special; she enjoys the day and lives it in a manner that glorifies the Lord. A stand up person is a person who rises daily to carry out his responsibilities. If we do our duty today then tomorrow will turn out just fine. Though people have been predicting the end of the world for a long time, Jesus makes it clear that this is not possible. We were not consulted when the world was created. And it is not our place to know how and when it will come to an end. We have the Holy Spirit of God and thus we have the means to learn all that we need to learn. It is wise to expect the Lord anytime now and to be ready at all times. Today we should prepare as if we expect Jesus to return tomorrow.

Prayer: Holy Spirit, please help me to stay vigilant and to be always ready so that the Lord will find me laboring in His vineyard when He returns.

November 17

—⊙⊙—

Surely, goodness and mercy shall follow me all the days of my life.

Psalm 23:6

Reflection: God asks that we be merciful with each other. Jesus once spoke of a king who forgave the debts of his head servant. Rather than pass on the forgiveness to those beneath him, the same servant was strict with the people who were indebted to him. Jesus made it clear that when the king found out how his forgiven servant was treating others, the king was not impressed. Much mercy and forgiveness we have received from God and, in turn, we are to show mercy and forgiveness to each other. A soft heart draws people to us and wins enemies over.

Prayer: Father God, let all those I come across say of me that I am kind and a forgiving person. May I always remember to pass on Your mercy in all my dealings.

November 18

———◁◦▷———

And when was it that we saw You sick or in prison and visited You?

Matthew 25:39

Reflection: Many of us would not hesitate to offer assistance to a rich or powerful person. But what about helping those who are down and out? It is interesting that Jesus mentioned the sick and the imprisoned and not mansions and palaces, as places to visit. The reason is that Jesus is more concerned about the forgotten ones. Hospitals and prisons are places where there is a lot of pain and suffering. We think of the sick as innocent people, and prison as a place for the guilty. Yet for Jesus, both places are worthy of our time. These are places where love and hope are much needed. And as Jesus demonstrated, both the rich and the poor are saved by the grace of God. The imagery here is powerful.

Prayer: Lord, help me to never forget my brothers and sisters in hospitals and in prisons. Today in my prayer, I will remember those people.

November 19

So put away all malice and all deceit and hypocrisy and envy and all slander. Like newborn infants, long for the pure spiritual milk, that by it you may grow up into salvation – if indeed you have tasted that the Lord is good. As you come to Him, a living stone rejected by men but in one sight of God chosen and precious, you yourselves like living stones are being built up as a spiritual house, to be a holy priesthood, to offer spiritual sacrifices acceptable to God through Jesus Christ.

1 Peter 2:1-25

Reflection: Many of us turn to God because we do not reside in the palaces of the world. We turn to God at low points in life. Jesus was rejected in part because he was often in the company of the powerless. God often chooses the lowly people of the world to carry His message. We are the lowly ones and by being obedient to God we become God's messengers. What God asks of us is what a good parent would ask of a child – for us to be decent and kind to one another. Our conscience is good and pure because it is built by the Holy Spirit. Have you tasted that the Lord is good? If so why not draw even closer?

Prayer: Spirit of God, strengthen my heart as You help me to discard all the terrible things I have learned since birth. Today, I rejoice that You have elected me, to carry out the message of Jesus to those around me.

November 20

―◦―

I love you, O Lord, my strength.

Psalm 18:1

Reflection: To love God is the ultimate feeling in life. To love God is to respect God and to respect other people. All around us we see evidence of God's love for us. Our family, our friends, nature, forgiveness of sins through Jesus, the gift of the Holy Spirit, gifts and blessings from strangers in times of need, the work we do, the people we meet, – these are just a few of the ways that God blesses us. It is out of love that God does not allow us to perish for our wickedness; instead, God's hand is outstretched to guide us back to Him. This is the ultimate love. Those who meditate on God constantly tell us that anything good in us comes from God. Will you learn to love God?

Prayer: Spirit of God, remove from me all that prevents me from loving my God with all of my heart and soul. Today and every day I will marvel in the love of God.

November 21

And I will be a father to you, and you shall be sons
and daughters to me, says the Lord Almighty.
2 Corinthians 6:18

Reflection: One of the hardest things for a parent to do is to boot
a wayward child out of the house. But having found the strength to
do so, a good parent will pray fervently for the welfare of the child.
The above verse is a reminder that we have been separated from God
who created us to be His children. The verse reminds us that we have
become like the prodigal son who wandered off because he wanted
to be free to do as he pleased. But the prodigal son soon realized that
all he ever wanted was already at his parents' house, and that no one
loved him more than his parents. Our ultimate destiny is to live as
God's children.

Prayer: God, thank You for being my Father and for teaching me how
to be a good child and a good parent to my children. I pray that I will
live as a child of God.

November 22

———◦———

Whoever troubles his own household will inherit the
wind, and the fool will be servant to the wise of heart.
Proverbs 11:29

Reflection: There are many ways to bring trouble to one's household. Violence, adultery, drug or alcohol abuse bring great troubles to families and the effects of these vices may stain the family for generations. We are loved and sustained by God who created us to build happy families. It is our duty to do all that we can to nurture our family with love and wisdom. The statistics are very disheartening regarding family turmoil arising from unfaithfulness and other issues. A family that prays together stays together because a family that prays together is one that respects the laws of God. Happy family life begins with parents who live as Jesus taught. Wise parents do not indoctrinate or pressure their children to attend Church or even to believe in God. A parent that is open and honest about his faith and is willing to allow a child to follow her conscience, is following the Will of God.

Prayer: Father, may I be a model of love, wisdom, and forgiveness to my family. May I never pressure my children against what their conscience teaches them. Today I will teach my child that all people are loved by God.

November 23

---◦◦◦---

I truly understand that God shows no partiality, but in every nation anyone who fears Him and does what is right is acceptable to Him.

Acts 10:34

Reflection: Ancient people, and even people in some parts of the world today think of God as their God alone. The reality is that there is no "us" and "them" so far as God is concerned. There is only one human species, with a common origin. Our genes contain bits and pieces of each other. The idea of a 'pure' race is something that exists only in the minds of misguided persons. We are all children of God, called to live as one people. This verse reminds us that we come to God as individuals and not as part of a church or a congregation or even a nation. Our individual choices define us, and define our relationship with God.

Prayer: Lord, help me to see everyone as my brother and sister, so that I may show no partiality or favoritism or promote racist ideology that divides people.

November 24

I have finished the race, and I have remained faithful.
2 Timothy 4:7

Reflection: In a running race only the front runners win prizes. But in life we all win no matter where we start or where we finish. This is because the race was won on our behalf long ago by Jesus. What is required of us is contrite hearts and a desire to accept the grace offered us. We do so by allowing the Holy Spirit to vanquish wickedness from our lives. And while we may be hard pressed to say that we have remained faithful, we should be able to say that we put our best effort into life. We understand that our journey exposes in us those things that are defective in us so that we might grow in spirit. And with our consent, the Holy Spirit uses our defects to open new doors and to impart new teachings, so that others will see a reflection of the Lord in us. And when we return to the Father, we can enter into His eternal grace.

Prayer: Spirit of God, strengthen my feet and focus my gaze so that I may not be distracted from my goal. I pray that my Master will say to me, "well done faithful servant."

—⊙⊃—

For our present troubles are small and won't last long.
Yet they produce for us a glory that vastly outweighs
them and will last forever!

2 Corinthians 4:17

Reflection: A loving parent does not always shield a child from the consequences of his action. Consequences are what enables the child to understand which choices are desirable and which ones are to be avoided. As adults, troubles come to us from the choices we make. Troubles can also come from choices made by those who came before us. Choices made by other people affect our food, the environment we live in, and even the water we drink. But trouble can make us better people especially when we are willing to stop and reflect regularly. Troubles make us seek knowledge, even scientific knowledge, and to use it wisely. This is all part of God's plan.

Prayer: Father, teach me to always learn the easy way, and not always through troubles. Teach me to seek Your guidance in prayer constantly.

November 26

---◦◦◦---

All wrongdoing is sin, and there is sin that does not lead to death.

1 John 5:17

Reflection: We think of sin as big sin and small sin. Most of the time we do not have to worry about big sins. But what about the small ones. Picking up our dog's litter in the park, men lifting up toilet seat, returning phone calls, getting to work on time, hanging up clothes, are these things that God cares about? The fact is that for our psychological wellbeing and for our spiritual growth, small things do matter. Our level of integrity is a good indicator of how serious we are about following Jesus, we are called to acquire self-discipline so that we do not neglect the small things.

Prayer: Spirit of God, help to take even the small things in my life seriously, especially the promises that I make to other people.

November 27

Rejoice with me for I have found my sheep that was lost.
Just so, I tell you, there will be more joy in heaven over
one sinner who repents than over ninety-nine righteous
persons who need no repentance.

Luke 15:6-7

Reflection: Jesus in this verse, demonstrates the extent of God's love for us. The ninety nine righteous persons in heaven were no doubt working with the Holy Spirit for the conversion of one sinner. Despite having these righteous children with Him, God never forgot the one that was missing. This is why we are not destroyed the moment we start to do wrong. Instead, all of creation conspires to help us to see the errors of our choices and to help us make better choices. God's love and mercy is so great, that if we have one breath left, and we use it to repent, we will be forgiven.

Prayer: May heaven rejoice today because I will answer the call of God.

November 28

With the measure you use, it will be measured to you.

Matthew 7:1

Reflection: It is difficult for us to ask God not to judge us by the same standard we apply to those who offend us. If we are harsh or unforgiving we may be inviting God to be harsh and unforgiving with us. A wise person, then, is easy on other people. Few people are more annoying than a person who condemns others and is just as guilty. Hypocrisy is something to be avoided. Condemning others for something that we ourselves are guilty of, or blaming others for things beyond their control, does not draw people to God. As Jesus said to those who wished to stone a woman caught in adultery, "Let him without sin, cast the first stone". The conscience of a merciful person pleads for mercy.

Prayer: Thank You, Father, for being so forgiving. Help me to always remember that I too rely on Your grace so that I may not go around condemning others.

November 29

You have already won a victory over those people because the Spirit who lives in you is greater than the Spirit who lives in the world.

1 John 4:4

Reflection: The Spirit in us is from God. But the Spirit bent on destroying the world and bent on creating misery is an evil spirit, known as Satan or the devil. Devotion to prayer is an invitation to the Spirit of God to abide in us. God's Spirit is never limited in power and so, if we are led by God, then all things become possible. This verse reminds us that the enemy of God has no hold on us unless we invite him into our life, by participating in things that bring hurt to others or to our self. So let us relax and trust in the Spirit of God within us. Jesus by his death defeated death and so not even death has a hold on us when we abide in Jesus. Our victory comes from the fact that we have been chosen by God to be His children.

Prayer: Father, help me to live each day knowing and trusting in the Spirit that You have sent to guide me. Today I will rejoice in the knowledge that God the Father made me to be His child.

November 30

Be dressed for action and have your lamps lit; be like those who are waiting for their masters to return from the wedding banquet, so that they may open the door for him as soon as he comes and knocks.

Luke 12:35-36

Reflection: People who organize war know the advantage of taking the enemy by surprise. Jesus is telling us in this verse that a wise person is always prepared and is never taken by surprise. Let our repentance begin the moment we hear God's voice. If we wait another day, it might be too late. God is so merciful that if we repented on our deathbed after a life of disobedience, we will be forgiven. But who knows when that hour will come? This is why Jesus tells us over and over again to always be prepared. We should form a habit of prayer and devotion. Daily, we face temptations and bad habits and so daily we must come before the Lord to renew our strength so that we are awake and alert when the Master returns.

Prayer: Holy Spirit, create in me a yearning for goodness and for devotion and may I not take your patience for granted. Help me to stay alert at all times so that my Master's joy might be complete when He returns.

December 1

Fools say in their heart, "There is no God."

Psalm 14:1

Reflection: From a Christian point of view, the evidence for the existence of God is overwhelming. However it is not inconceivable, that there are people who in good conscience have doubts. But for anyone to claim that God does not exist, is highly presumptuous. Who has searched the universe and learned the secrets of the stars? It is true that the idea that God exists is astounding. But it is also just as amazing that humans can exist. Yet here we are. Sometimes the problem with accepting God's existence, has to do with the fact, that it is difficult for us to accept our own existence. But our circumstance in this regard is no different from that of an ant, who is attempting to understand what it means to be human. While our minds cannot capture the essence of God, we are able to perceive the presence of God in our lives. The way to God is not through intellectual debates, but through living the teachings of Jesus. One way to God, is by living the truths hardwired into us at birth.

Prayer: Father, the more that I strive to be holy and to be loving, the clearer I see You in the world. Help me Father, to stay focused on living as Jesus taught.

December 2

To you has been given the secret of the kingdom of God,
but for those outside, everything comes in parables, in
order that 'they may indeed look but not perceive, and
may indeed listen, but not understand' so that they
might return and be forgiven.

Mark 4:11-12

Reflection: The Lord was not running a secret society. When he referred to those "outside", he was talking about self-righteous people, those people who saw no need for redemption. Lack of repentance, (demonstrated by a change in attitude and behavior), not only drives a wedge between us and God, it makes us reject God. When we act contrary to the guidance of the Holy Spirit, we find it very difficult to turn to God. And those who do not submit to the Will of God, will misapprehend His nature. One consequence of disobedience, is that our conscience does not allow us to turn to God until we are ready to repent. And so, one measure of how repentant we are is the extent of our prayer life. The more we pray, the less we are tempted and the more we are remorseful. No one who is open to the Will of God, can ridicule our faith.

Prayer: Father God, I have come to recognize that my knowledge of You comes from what You reveal to me. Help me to remain open and humble so I might not seek to become my own god.

December 3

Truly I tell you, this very day, this very night, before the cock crows twice, you will deny Me three times.
Matthew 26:34/ Mark 14:30

Reflection: Jesus said these words to Peter after he swore that he would never deny knowing Jesus. Peter loved Jesus and he was devoted to Him. But like the rest of us, he was weak and did not know it. So, when Peter vowed to never deny Jesus, he was sincere. But when someone accused Peter of being a follower of Jesus, he denied this to be the case. Like Peter, it is often during trials and tribulations that we come to learn more about our character. No person ever believed that he would become an addict when he first used alcohol or drugs. This is why it is good to pray, and to read Scripture, and to meditate regularly. We also must respect and fear sin, so we do not become too relaxed. Poor Peter, he was so sure of himself.

Prayer: Spirit of God, teach me about myself, and gently help me to understand my weaknesses. Help me to be on guard constantly so that I may not become complacent.

December 4

If we confess our sins, He is faithful and just and will forgive us our sins and will purify us from all unrighteousness.

1 John 1:9

Reflection: God knows our sins better than we remember them. The purpose of confession is not to tell God something new; it is to ensure that we come to terms with our past and renounce wickedness and to submit to the help of the Holy Spirit. To confess one's sins is to begin to understand who we are and how we can improve. Confession makes it easier to move on and to not keep repeating the same mistakes. Moreover, unconfessed sins eat away at our peace of mind and retard our spiritual growth. An old Scottish proverb says, "Confession is good for the soul"; this is true even though it is not a Biblical quote.

Prayer: Help me, Lord, to gently face up to who I am and help me to forgive myself as You forgive me.

December 5

I can do everything through Him who gives me strength.
Philippians 4:13

Reflection: You would think that a leisurely life under the sun, somewhere scenic would be very rewarding. But many people who have chosen this path often complain that their lives become dull and unexciting. They often have no desire to rise in the morning. On the other hand, people who choose to serve others tell us that they always find the strength to rise and are always motivated to get out there, working and helping. The conclusion then is that life is most fulfilling when we take our responsibility towards each other seriously. From the Christian point of view, we never have to worry about resources or about opportunities for service, if our desire is to assist others. The Holy Spirit strengthens and equips everyone in service of the Lord.

Prayer: Spirit of God, make my life meaningful and rewarding and help me to enjoy the tasks that the Father has laid out for me.

December 6

But blessed are your eyes, for they see: and your ears, for they hear.

Matthew 13:16

Reflection: Eyes and ears pass on information about the environment. What we do with the information depends on where we are in life. But even when two or more people are looking at the same thing they do not necessarily perceive the same thing. What we perceive about spirituality (and there is spirituality in everything in life), largely depends on how open we are to the teaching of the Holy Spirit. As we acquire God's wisdom, things we see or hear daily take on new meanings and fresh understanding emerges. As we grow spiritually, occurrences which we once never paid attention to or regarded as "coincidence" begin to point to the path for us. The Holy Spirit is so involved in our life that there really are no coincidences.

Prayer: Open my heart, Oh Lord, so that my stubbornness and desires might not block what You are revealing to me, help me to perceive as clearly as Your saints do.

December 7

I saw that under the sun the race is not to the swift, nor the battle to the strong, nor the bread to the wise, nor riches to the intelligent, nor favor to the skillful; but time and chance happen to them all.

Ecclesiastes 9:11

Reflection: This passage expresses one of the mysteries of God. Part of the issue here is that we often think we know who is a good person and who is deserving of this or that from God. We say things like so and so is a good person because he does a lot for charity. But it is not really for us to judge anyone good or bad. Only God knows the true circumstance of each person and only God is in a position to judge, good or bad. A boy who grows up in a fatherless home with a troubled mother may not be held to the same standard of character by God than a boy from a loving two-parent home. If we appear to have been dealt an unfortunate hand by life, God makes it up to us in other ways. And so the race is not always won by those we think of as good. We will never fully understand God's relationship with other people.

Prayer: Spirit of God, teach me about myself and help me to stop making assumptions about who is good or who is bad. I recognize that I will never know enough to be able to judge anyone fairly, this is Your domain.

December 8

───◦◦◦───

You shall love the Lord, your God, with all your heart
and with all your soul and with all your mind.

Matthew 22:37

Reflection: Parents know how good it feels to be loved by their children. Our love is all that we have to give back to our Father. But the love of God is not something one can fake or something that we can think our way into. Love comes from the heart. We love God after we come to appreciate that God loved us first. We see many examples in the Bible of people who showed their appreciation to Jesus, by loving Him. Mary loved Jesus because Jesus raised her brother Lazarus from the dead. She expressed her love by pouring expensive perfume on His feet and wiping His feet with her hair. Another time, a leper that Jesus healed came and laid at His feet. Can you think of reasons to love God?

Prayer: Father God, I love You because so many times you have delivered me from the depths of despair and plucked me from the grave. You have blessed me beyond my imagination and I cannot thank You enough. Above all I love You because You loved me so much that You gave up Your only Son to die for me.

December 9

This is love: not that we loved God, but that He loved us and sent His Son as an atoning sacrifice for our sins. Dear friends, since God so loved us, we also ought to love one another.

1 John 4:10

Reflection: If Jesus is the visible image of the living God, then it is easy to love a God who became one of us, and at moments in His life, divested Himself of heavenly powers so that He could experience pain. If we love goodness, then we would have no difficulty loving God. The command from God is that we are to love one another, even to love those who may be difficult to love. Yes, there is pain and suffering in life and yes, there is much that we do not understand. But our pain is similar to the pain that a child experiences while growing up with parents who lovingly corrects the child when it is necessary to do so. This is why every time we look back at our life, we can always say: "the pain we went through has been worth it".

Prayer: Father, thank You so much for loving me. Teach me love as only You can so that I may love You with all of my heart and soul.

December 10

Discipline always seems painful rather than pleasant at the time, but later it yields the peaceful fruit of righteousness to those who have been trained by it.

Hebrews 12:11

Reflection: We can quibble over whether God punishes us when we sin or whether mental anguish always comes from sin or disobedience. What is certain is that we suffer, and that many times we cause our own suffering by making the wrong choices. If a bad choice that we make is not followed by consequences, most of us would hardly pay attention. Where would we be if God simply allowed us to do whatever we want whenever we want, with no consequences? One reason that tyrants and despots emerge in the world is because they are accountable to no one. The laws of God have been designed to ensure fair play on earth and to ensure as much fulfillment as possible for us all. God included discipline in our world so that we might be guided towards goodness.

Prayer: Spirit of God, thank You for counting me worthy to be disciplined, rather than to be discarded. Teach me to learn to discipline myself so that I might not be disciplined solely by life experiences.

December 11

The Lord is my rock, my fortress, and my deliverer, my
God, my rock, in whom I take refuge.

2 Samuel 22:3

Reflection: In Jesus, Christians stand on an immovable rock, in an impregnable fortification surrounded by angels who deliver us in times of troubles. In Jesus we stand on love and truth and so that evil cannot torment us. We all experience good days and bad days. Our thoughts are sometimes cheerful and sometimes gloomy. Many of these highs and lows happen because we do not hold firmly to the promise of God. Jesus emerged from a fast in the desert tired, hungry and thirsty, but He never succumbed to temptations because He had been steadfast in prayer. A life built on hope in Jesus will not be pushed around by the trials of daily living.

Prayer: Father God, the life of Your Son Jesus showed what is possible when we are faithful to Your Word and when we pray regularly. May the Holy Spirit grant me the desire to yearn for the spirituality that Jesus taught His disciples.

December 12

Let us therefore hold boldly to the throne of grace, that we may obtain mercy and find grace to help in time of need.

Hebrews 4:16

Reflection: In times of need, it would be nice to have the assurance of mercy and grace. This verse reminds us that if we form a habit of abiding in God, then whenever trouble comes our way, it will find us hanging on to the throne of God. When we pray regularly we are holding on to the throne of God and in so doing it becomes difficult for us to be separated from our faith. This is not to suggest that we earn forgiveness, or earn the Grace of God. But if we fail to abide in God, our faith weakens and we are liable to be tormented by trouble. On the other hand if our faith is steadfast then in times of trouble, we will not experience the mental anguish which lack of faith brings. No one who pleads faithfully at the feet of Jesus is turned away.

Prayer: Spirit of God, grant me a place at the feet of Jesus so that I may sing God's praise forever with all the saints and angels. Today I will claim the mercy and grace granted me by the Christ of God.

December 13

No one has ever seen God. But if we love each other, God lives in us, and His love is brought to full expression in us. And God has given us His Spirit as proof that we live in Him and He in us.

1 John 4:12

Reflection: A lot of our troubles come from our thoughts. We let our imagination run wild as we imagine terrible things happening to us. Medical students are typically certain that they suffer from every ailment imaginable. The rest of us surprisingly, even when we draw close to God, are just as worried that something may be wrong with us. Jesus tells us that there is hope for all worrywarts. If we form a habit of regular devotion, we will learn to trust in God and our worries becomes less over time. Worry is a signal that we are letting things get out of control and that we need to trust more in God.

Prayer: Take away my worries, Oh Lord, and help me to relax in Your loving grace. I will cast all my fears and worries unto the feet of Jesus.

December 14

O Lord, in the morning You hear my voice; in the morning, I plead my case to You and watch.

Psalm 5:3

Reflection: Many people think that faith is a way for Christians to avoid making hard choices in life. This is not true. It is in fact when we begin to have faith that we realize how much discipline is required to live as Jesus taught. Jesus was always praying and we must do the same. The best way to start the day is to put on the armor of God in the morning. Prayer helps us to call to mind our goals and inviting the Holy Spirit in to guide and watch over us as we start the day, can be the difference between a peaceful productive day and a tumultuous day. When we start out by reaffirming our goals and ideals and seek the help and guidance of our Father, we have a good chance of being faithful to the spirit within us. God smiles and blesses those who come to Him day and night. No one is more merciful than our Father.

Prayer: Father, help me to always remember the benefits of prayer and the benefits of always examining my heart so that I may start each day with Your blessings.

December 15

*Humble yourselves, therefore, under the mighty hand of
God so that at the proper time he may exalt you.*

1 Peter 5:6

Reflection: The amazing thing about rich people is that many of them
have humble beginnings. Whatever station we find ourselves in life,
it is important to do the best we can with what we have so that God is
able to trust us with more. If we happen to occupy a high position then
all the more reason to learn humility. A king that is humble is much
loved by his people. But a tyrant is cursed by the people. A servant of
the Lord who is humble is trusted with great gifts. On the other hand
if we occupy a not so desirable position, we still have a responsibility
to be diligent. Rich or poor, we are to be humble before other people.
God is more likely to exalt humble people.

Prayer: Spirit of God, help me to recognize the tricks of the devil
as I go about my daily chores and lead me not into temptation but
deliver me from every evil. I pray that I remember to remain humble
no matter how well things go for me.

December 16

Nothing in all creation will ever be able to separate us from the love of God that is revealed in Christ Jesus our Lord.

Romans 8:39

Reflection: The love that God has for us does not depend on how well behaved we are. The Bible tells us that we are God's highest creation, and Jesus tells us to call God Father. We see then that we have a special relationship with God that is unbreakable. God is forever faithful. He made us so that He can love us and even when we are disobedient or deny Him, the Holy Spirit continues to sustain us and waits patiently for us to have a change of heart.

Prayer: Father, may I never be separated from Your love and may I come to love You with all of my heart and soul. Thank You for Your Grace.

December 17

The *wisdom from above is first pure, then peaceable, gentle, willing to yield, full of mercy and good fruits, without a trace of partiality or hypocrisy.*

James 3:17

Reflection: This verse lists some of the attributes of God that Jesus mirrored when He was here on Earth. And it is these attributes which draw us to God because deep down, we have similar qualities in us and so we recognize them as good. And we admire these traits when we see them in other people. People who misunderstand the origin and context of the Old Testament often say that God is a vengeful God. This is not true. "I am the truth," Jesus said. And the truth is that even the most ardent atheist would confess that Jesus is the embodiment of love, peace, and compassion. We love God not just because God loved us first but also because God is good to us.

Prayer: Father, help me to take my commitment to seek wisdom, seriously so that I never become complacent. I pray that I will influence everyone that I come across to think about Jesus.

December 18

Christ came as a servant to the Jews to show that God has kept the promises he made to their famous ancestors. Christ also came so that Gentiles would praise God for being kind to them.

Romans 15:8-9

Reflection: Paul himself a Jew, in this letter, reminds us that Christianity owes its origins to the Jewish faith. In the above letter Paul tells us that God chose Christ so that Jews would bring honor to God and be the first ones to have hope because of Jesus. And so today, we thank God that through Jesus, salvation has come to all who desire God. People who reject our faith often argue that our God is a tribal God, a God of the Jews, who care little about other people. If this were true, there would be no other people on earth except Jewish people. The fact is that throughout scripture, we read that those who sought God found God, regardless of their tribal origin, and that those who were unrepentant in their wickedness were never favored by God, regardless of their origin. Our faith is that God is the Father of all people and that we come to God as individual repentant creatures. Christ died for the sins of all humanity.

Prayer: Father I thank you that because of Your son I too can call you Father. May the choices I make daily remind others of your Grace and Love.

December 19

Everyone then who hears these words of Mine and acts on them will be like a wise man who built his house upon rock.

Matthew 7:24

Reflection: A house whose foundation is anchored to a rock will withstand the ravages of the weather. And so we too, if we place our hope and trust in Jesus, we will not be subject to many of the anxieties which life produces. We are often told by atheists that what we hold sacred in Jesus is actually a myth. But what they regard as myth, we call love and wisdom. The teachings of Jesus reflect goodness. The words of Jesus appeal to the goodness within us even if we have difficulty living up to these words. And so if we aspire to have the best possible life, there is no better teacher than Jesus.

Prayer: Spirit of God, help me to build the best foundation possible on the Rock of Ages, Jesus, so that storms of temptations will never wash away my faith.

December 20

Anxiety in a man's heart weighs it down, but an encouraging word makes it glad.

Proverbs 12:25

Reflection: There are those who delight in bringing good news. These are the peacemakers, the volunteers, many professionals such as doctors and nurses, political leaders and many more. And there are those who do not mind creating bloodshed. The outbreak of violence creates anxiety and this weighs down the human spirit. Easily the best way to acquire long-term peace of mind is to trust in God and to stay away from all manners of wickedness. Small evil disturbs the mind little and big evil disturbs the mind much. Jesus gave us the Good News and so we too ought to delight in words and actions which encourage other people.

Prayer: Father, may I always delight in bringing hope and good news to everyone I meet. Today I will say nice and encouraging things to those I come across.

December 21

God's love was revealed among us in this way: God sent His only Son into the world so that we might live through Him.

1 John 4:9

Reflection: The cornerstone of our faith is the historical record and confirmation by the Holy Spirit, of the life of Jesus on earth. Jesus was a human and He experienced pain and suffering. And as a human, He showed that complete obedience to God is possible. As a Spirit, he bore our sins and defeated death, which is the destiny of sinners. This is part of the creation plan, part of the growth of our humanity.

Prayer: Father God, your servant Stephen prayed for those who stoned him because he believed that they did not know what they were doing. Help me to bear the derision and ridicule of those who seek to deny Your existence.

December 22

The Lord is not slow in keeping His promise as some understand slowness. He is patient with you, not wanting anyone to perish, but everyone to come to repentance.

1 Peter 3:9

Reflection: Our life is not over the moment we sin. We are given ample opportunities to repent and to learn. Before we ask, before we speak, God already understands and God already knows what we have done. Our prayer to God helps us to focus and to begin to appreciate what keeps us apart from God. If the response to our prayers seems slow in coming, this is only because it takes human time for the Holy Spirit to reform our attitude so that having been saved, we do not return to the same sins. God works from the inside out to bring about a change of attitude. We are changed by accepting the opportunity to confront the past and to reject it. How much time this takes depends on us. On the other hand if we were judged as soon as we did wrong, then no one would survive to learn and to repent. But no one knows the day or the hour, so a wise person does not wait to experience God's displeasure before turning to God.

Prayer: Father, help me to be patient, to be joyful, and to never lose heart as You work with me. I pray to reflect upon my shortcomings so that the Holy Spirit might help me to do away with them.

December 23

---∘∘∘---

My grace is sufficient for you for My power is made perfect in weakness.

2 Corinthians 12:9

Reflection: This was the response given to the Apostle Paul after he prayed to God for healing. Paul tells us that he had a thorn on his side and it was left there to keep him humble after God had entrusted him with knowledge. This implies that had Paul managed to be sufficiently humble to serve as God wanted him to do, the thorn may have been removed. Scripture was written for our benefit, so that we can learn without having to stumble first. Paul would advise each of us to abide in the Lord and to allow the Holy Spirit to work in us. The other point that Paul would make is that we can experience joy, no matter what conditions we are faced with. There may be times when the grace of God supports an ailment which fosters God's Will. God knows us more than we know ourselves. God knows our weakness and so there may be times when our weakness is so overwhelming that we need a constant reminder of who we are, rather than a perfect healing. When we pray for healing, we may be given God's grace and peace. Whatever the outcome of prayer we must believe that God has done His will.

Prayer: Father, may I always find peace in Your will even as I pray for healing. Today I will revel in the Grace of God.

December 24 — Christmas Eve

The name of the Lord is a strong tower, the righteous run to it and are safe.

Proverbs 18:10

Reflection: There is power in the name of Jesus, whose birth most Christians celebrate at this season. The type of power that we cannot fully grasp but which can be readily experienced first-hand. Alcoholics Anonymous and Narcotics Anonymous are two effective organizations inspired by the teachings of God. Many lives have been saved in the name of Jesus. The world has been civilized by the teachings of Jesus. Most people are drawn to people who follow Jesus and the countries that are built on the teachings of Jesus. These countries attract the most refugees in the world and provide most of the charity in the world. Christian teachings have turned wild superstitious people into decent peace-loving people.

Prayer: Lord, shield me with Your love and may those fleeing from the hands of the wicked find refuge in my country and in Your teachings. Today my heart will be with those who are fleeing persecution and violence.

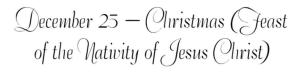

December 25 — Christmas (Feast of the Nativity of Jesus Christ)

Remember that you were at that time without Christ, being aliens from the commonwealth of Israel, and strangers to the covenant of promise, having no hope and without God in the world.

Ephesians 2: 11-13

Reflection: Abraham put his faith in the living God and became a father of many nations. Ancient Israelites believed and trusted in God and their hope sustained them in spite of the overwhelming odds they faced. This verse reminds us that we owe our redemption to Jesus. Until the Holy Birth of Jesus (which we commemorate on this Christmas Day, the Feast of the Nativity), the world worshipped idols, often sacrificing humans and engaging in other acts of wickedness. Paul is telling the Ephesians and the rest of us that we now share in the promise and hope that God first gave to the Israelites.

Prayer: Father, thank You that You have set out a path for me to return to You in the name of Jesus. Today my heart rejoices that You have counted me worthy to be redeemed from sin, and that You came into this world, born as an infant in human form, in order to save me.

December 26 – Feast of St. Stephen the First Martyr (Protomartyr)

Stephen, full of grace and power, did great wonders and signs among the people.

Acts 6:8

Reflection: Stephen was so full of love and compassion that he begged God for power to do wonders for the very people stoning him to death. Where did Stephen's love come from? Why was he able to keep praying even as he was dying? "Lord, forgive them, for they know not what they do," he said as stones landed on him. Could we too do what Stephen did? The answer is that yes we can, with the Holy Spirit, everything is possible. Stephen became empowered by being receptive to the Holy Spirit. When we are obedient to God, we are rewarded with a loving heart and grace that can turn pain into joy.

Prayer: Spirit of God, use me to do wonders so that my friends and family will witness Your love and mercy. Help me to bring a smile to the face of everyone I meet today.

December 27

And when he came to the place, he said to them, Pray
that you may not enter into temptation.

Luke 22:40

Reflection: Jesus demonstrated to us that it is possible to resist temptations. As a human Jesus experienced the same temptations that we encounter daily. But Jesus was always praying and so Jesus was strong. Indeed it is not easy for the children of God to gravely sin. The Holy Spirit puts obstacles, teachings, and warnings on the road to sin. But in the end, we maintain free will to climb over these hurdles and to engage in sinful acts, if this is our desire. Gracious God delivers us from evil in times of weakness.

Prayer: Spirit of God, strengthen my resolve so that I will always embrace Your deliverance from sin. I pray to be strengthened against sin just as Jesus was strengthened.

December 28

———◦○◦———

For our struggle is not against flesh and blood, but against the rulers, against the authorities, against the powers of this dark world and against the spiritual forces of evil in the heavenly realms.

Ephesians 6:12

Reflection: This passage highlights the fact that the evil one is the directing minds in many of the world's schemes. There are institutions, many legal, which exist only to exploit human weakness for personal gain. Just like there are those who make themselves available to be used by the Spirit of God, there are also those who chose to do the work of Satan. Evil spirits promote things which destroy people and families. When we engage in these things, we become exposed to bad intrusive thoughts and we lose our focus. Those around us suffer and we too suffer. Temptation is a spiritual warfare and it is only by abiding in the Lord that we overcome it. The Bible tells us that if we resist the devil, he will flee. Hallelujah.

Prayer: There is so much in my life that I do not fathom. Thank you, Jesus, that Your death and suffering has liberated me. I pray to avoid things and places which promote exploitation and take me away from Jesus.

December 29

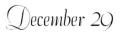

For God did not give us a spirit of timidity, but a spirit
of power, of love and of self-discipline.

2 Timothy 1:7

Reflection: We have all known fear and doubt, both of which are tools of the devil. But the devil only has a hold on us if we let him. Love drives out fear and keeps the devil away, and when we do the work that God has for us, we grow in love and in understanding. God has a solution for everything that troubles us or causes us to fear, we must never forget this. Yes, we sometimes find ourselves in predicaments which appear so daunting that we cannot imagine a happy solution. The prophet Isaiah is telling us that nothing is impossible for God. Rather than fear, or doubt, or worry, we should just pray and pray and pray. If God were to feel pride (which He clearly does not as it is sinful), it would likely occur whenever we put our trust in Him.

Prayer: Father, as I struggle against demons in my life, I know that You are always at my side guiding me through. I pray for continued strength and protection.

December 30

"We give thanks to God always for all of you, constantly mentioning you in our prayers, remembering before our God and Father your work of faith and labor of love and steadfastness of hope in our Lord Jesus Christ.

1 Thessalonians 1:1-3

Reflection: When it comes down to it, our main issue in life is lack of faith in the existence of a benevolent God. Yet when we do what Jesus teaches things improve remarkably for us and our faith in God grows. How many people can say they delight in knocking on God's door day and night only to be turned away? How many people put in the effort required to submit to the voice of the Spirit within each of us? How many people delight in the worship of God? These are the means with which to acquire faith. When we truly have faith we would not fear and we would never lack the motivation to be there for each other. Effort is required for spiritual growth. We are called to do our part in creating the world.

Prayer: Father, thank You for my conscience. Help me to never be satisfied until Your will becomes my will. Thank You God, for all that You do for me.

December 31 - Feast Day of St. Sylvester

For me, to live is Christ…

Philippians 1:21

Reflection: A life without a spiritual purpose is not very fulfilling. The soul that ignores its spirituality is always restless and prone to questionable behavior. There is no lasting joy in material goods. Those who have managed to acquire a lot of wealth often lament the emptiness they feel unless they nurture their spirituality. Perhaps it is spiritual emptiness that makes some people climb dangerous mountains, jump out of airplanes, and others engage in risky behaviors. This is not to suggest that people who engage in risky ventures lack spirituality. Jesus was a worker. It was through service and obedience that Jesus found fulfillment. Notice that the happiest people are also the people who work hard to make life better for others. What it means to live in Christ is doing the things that Jesus did.

Prayer: Lord, may I discover You in my work, in my play, in my family, and even in those that I disagree with. I pray to always abide in the Lord.

ABOUT THE AUTHOR

Elvis A. Iginla is lawyer who lives in Edmonton, Canada.

CPSIA information can be obtained at www.ICGtesting.com
Printed in the USA
LVOW11s2304290116

472414LV00002B/28/P